Sister Circle Handbook

Balancing the Joy of Friendship with Your God-Given Gifts

Book Five of

The Sister Circle Series

Nancy Moser & Brenda Josee

Overland Park, KS

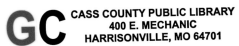

• • •

To be thanked . . .

We would like to acknowledge the wonderful book *Discover Your God Given Gifts* by Don and Katie Fortune which helped the two of us discover ours.

The Sister Circle Handbook

ISBN-10: 0998620602
ISBN: 978-0-9986206-0-2

Mustard Seed Press
10605 W. 165 Street
Overland Park, KS 66221

All Scripture quotations are taken from The Holy Bible, New Living Translation Bible

Front cover design by Mustard Seed Press

Contents

• Introductions •
(Who We Are)

When you opened the cover of this book, you probably didn't expect to find two women eager to meet you. But here we are — Nancy and Brenda — you can't get rid of us now. You can't see us, you can't touch us, but if you listen carefully as you read, you will hear us. We've laughed, cried, sung, prayed (a lot), and worked really hard to create the *Sister Circle Handbook* with you in mind. Have we presumed on our sisterhood? Probably. But only because we're a lot like you.

Brenda lives on the West Coast and is a grandmother. She likes gardening, cooking (she's called the Pillsbury Dough-Girl), pastel colors, old movies with predict-able plotlines, hot weather, long walks, the smell of citrus, and planning other people's lives.

Nancy lives in the Midwest and has three grown children and seven grandchildren. She hates gardening. She likes to eat out, intense colors, complex suspenseful movies, snow, no exercise whatsoever, the smell of cinnamon, and creating make-believe lives for the characters in her novels.

We both like lots of real butter, Broadway tunes, scented bath stuff, pretty stationery, and not washing windows. We're more the same than different. Like you, we want the same things: happiness, love, contentment, fulfillment, and an extra helping of sweets that won't go to our hips. We can help each other get these things because we're in this together.

Women have a unique capacity to bond. We can connect with the woman in front of us at the market or exchange child-rearing tips with someone we just met in an elevator. Men don't do this, and, more amazingly, don't want to (they don't know what they're missing). The truth is, God made us this way. So enjoy it — enjoy each other, and enjoy the *Sister Circle*

Handbook. Let's have fun with the to-dos, how-tos, and good news about being a sister in Christ.

Inside you'll find a place to do a little self-exploration (put on your pith-helmet, we're digging deep here). You'll pinpoint a few of your God-given gifts and hopefully discover ways to use them more effectively in everyday life as you live out your unique purpose. You'll find suggestions of things to do for yourself and for others, plus a section of party ideas to enjoy with your sisters. As the icing on the cake, we've included all the recipes mentioned in *The Sister Circle* novels. (What novels? See a teaser at the back of this book for the scoop).

In these pages we've tried to cover it all. The shopping, sex, and dentist appointments we'll leave to you.

• Get Ready! •
(Sister Circles)

"Wise words bring many benefits,
and hard work brings rewards."
Proverbs 12:14

Before you dive in it's time to find some helpful support for the journey. One way to do that is to form a Sister Circle.

If you ask women to check their calendars, they probably wouldn't look at many entries with anticipation. Not many of us put "friends" on the calendar — or if we do, we feel guilty. Yet most of us have a circle of friends. But how often do we get together? We usually meet for a specific reason: a bridal shower, a meeting to plan a school event, an evening of Bunko . . . But wouldn't it be nice to have a group of girlfriends whose main reason to get together was to cherish and nourish each other as sisters?

Sister Circles are all about looking beyond *me* to *we.* Social media has awakened a desire to connect face to face, to belong in a circle of friends we can see in person, not just chat with in some virtual cloud. When we do get together we're used to having structure. An agenda, a schedule, a goal. We've lost the joy of our grandmother's era, when women gathered and just talked. There weren't televisions, day planners, or e-mail. You met, bonded, and became a vital part of each other's lives. Sister Circles help us return to that simpler time. Times when we *shared* time.

We choose our friends because they satisfy our longing for companionship, stimulate our thinking, spark our creativity, know the location of the best sales . . . our motives are varied, and we may not even be able to pinpoint exactly why we like a certain someone. We don't need to analyze it. The fact there *is* a bond is all we need to know. They *do* something for our being. Hopefully, we *do* the something back.

We encourage you to gather the best of the best (friends, that is). How about having your friend from church meet your friend from work, your neighbor down the street, and the lady who does your hair? Old, young, professional, mommy . . . the only qualification for sisterhood is friendship. And consider this: A Sister Circle can be that one place where you don't have to be politically correct, a place you can talk about life *and* faith issues. What freedom! Have you noticed that the deepest friendships usually involve God? There's a reason for that.

The great thing about getting close to a group of women in a Sister Circle is that we can help each other find our purpose, accept our differences, and celebrate our individual strengths. There's a special balance between us. And we all know that the best growth is the growth that comes from loving each other through Him, right? How great is that?

A Sister Circle can be whatever you want it to be. It can change week to week or month to month. There's no formal structure. Our dream is for sisters to bond for life with their love of Christ as the glue that holds them together. To help get things started, here are a few common interests. Why not get together to:

- Read
- Cook (and eat!)
- Exercise (if you must)
- Scrapbook
- Share a Bible study
- Discuss the *Sister Circle Handbook* material
- Make jewelry or other craft items
- Quilt, knit, crochet, cross-stitch or create other handwork
- Share journaling or other writing
- Work on family genealogy
- Practice photography
- Help each other redecorate (I'll bring the paintbrush, you bring the paint remover)
- Paint or draw

- Share travelogues (don't groan)
- Shop (the one who finds the best bargain wins!)

See how easy it is? Make a list of the women in your life, pick up the phone, or send an old fashioned paper invitation or an online e-vite . Get together that first time and see what happens!

Once a month? Once a week? *It doesn't matter.*

Six women? Twelve? *It doesn't matter.*

Meet at church? In a house? In a park? At a coffee shop? *It doesn't matter.*

Sweeten the event with a plate of goodies, and you'll attain true perfection (store-bought is fine, we won't tell).

That's all it takes. The rest will come.

We would love to hear about your Sister Circle. Send us pictures and tell us about the fun you are having. We would like to know about all the "love and good deeds" of your sisterhood. (bookmoser@gmail.com or bjosee396@gmail.com)

The Sister Circle Pledge

I will hold tightly to my hope
that God can be trusted to keep His Promises.
I will think of ways to encourage my sisters
to outbursts of love and good deeds.
Paraphrase of Hebrews 10: 23-24

• • •

God's Word Says:

"Don't just pretend to love others.
Really love them. Hate what is wrong.
Hold tightly to what is good.
Love each other with genuine affection,
and take delight in honoring each other.
Never be lazy, but work hard and serve the Lord enthusiastically."
Romans 12:9-11

• What's Ahead •

As you can see, the *Sister Circle Handbook* is divided into 13 chapters. Each chapter delves into a topic that affects—or will affect—everyone at some time. If you have a sister who insists she knows nothing about the topics of "Disappointment" or "Loneliness," refrain from wanting to say, "Wanna bet?" Once you get going, she'll see the light.

It is not our intent to present an exhaustive look into each topic. Our desire is to present topics for discussion and stimulate your thinking. Women are creative and imaginative, and we believe that when you sincerely desire to enjoy time together, you will nurture each other and the Holy Spirit will guide you into exciting discoveries. The chapter topic is merely a starting point.

The chapters can be handled in many ways. If you'd like everyone to go through the chapter at home while they are alone, fill in the blanks, and then share their thoughts once you get together, that's fine. Or simply go through the chapter together. Have ladies volunteer to read aloud different sections. There are Scripture references, the text, discussion questions, and excerpts from *The Sister Circle* novels that illustrate the topics. At the end of each chapter, there are to-do ideas "For Me" and "For Others", things to do together or alone. Come up with different ideas, far more creative than ours.

Some ladies may not be at ease reading aloud. That's okay, too. We want everyone to feel comfortable so they will open up during the discussions. The logistics of who does what is far less important than the sharing.

So . . . open the book and ask for volunteers. Then let the chapters carry you along.

One more point: Respect your fellow sisters. There are

always a few who can't tell time. Start your get-togethers punctually. Don't worry about the late ones, they're used to playing catch-up. And be watchful toward the ending time of the gathering. If the discussion is good you can always continue on the same chapter next time. But if the discussion has digressed (as can happen in a group of lively ladies), it is your job as the Super Sister to proclaim "Whoa, Sisters! Rein it in!" Respect that people live busy lives and need to get home on time. That's an important part of being a Super Sister. They'll love you for it.

• The Sister Circle Novels •

We mentioned the excerpts from *The Sister Circle* novels . . . You might be saying, "Huh? What are those?" They are a series of four Christian novels that were the impetus for the *Sister Circle Handbook*. There's *The Sister Circle, Round the Corner, An Undivided Heart,* and *A Place to Belong.* They revolve around a Victorian boarding house where women of different backgrounds, personalities, and ages come together and bond as sisters in Christ. We have used excerpts from the novels to illustrate the different topics because, being fictional, they're safe. You can discuss exactly how the fictional character Tessa is being selfish and Mae is being too bossy without hurting their feelings. Use them rather than each other as examples. It's not necessary for you to read the novels to enjoy the *Sister Circle Handbook,* but if you choose to do so, let it happen. They are available in eBooks and print versions on Amazon. Each book has extensive discussion questions in the back, so they could be used at a later date for a book club.

Above all, remember this: a Sister Circle is not a *love me, give me, bless me* club, but it *is* a place to share blessings.

CHAPTER 1

• Let's Go! •
(Uncovering Your God-Given Gifts)

"Encourage each other. Live in harmony and peace.
Then the God of love and peace will be with you."
2 Corinthians 13:11

• • •

Every woman brings something special to the sisterhood. Only our awesome God could create us to be so distinctively unique. You (yes, you!) are a one-of-a-kind creation with a one-of-a-kind purpose. Instead of saying, "No, not me!" (in humility or even rebellion) grab something munchy and celebrate. You, dear sister, are special!

Yet as distinct and unique as we are, we share similar needs and struggles as we cope with what life drops on our doorstep (and that includes dealing with the morning news). Life, by its very nature, is diverse and requires a different approach at different times. It's kind of like shoes . . . you wouldn't wear stilettos to play tennis, would you? But let's face it, certain sisters are better at certain types of situations than others.

Why is that? Because God made us this way.

If you will bring everything you are and surrender it to Him, He will take everything you are and make it better — no plastic surgery, diet, or exercise required.

God has given us talents and abilities to do certain things well. He has also equipped us with personality traits that compliment those abilities. The passage in Romans 12:6-8 (below) highlights seven of the gifts God has so graciously handed out. As you continue to learn about these gifts in the Handbook, you will come to know yourself better — the you God created you to be. With that accomplished, you will see how you and your gifts can be best used to keep your Sister Circle balanced.

• • •

God's Word Says:

*"God has given us different gifts
for doing certain things well.
So if God has given you the ability to prophesy,
speak out with as much faith as God has given you.
If your gift is serving others, serve them well.
If you are a teacher, teach well.
If your gift is to encourage others, be encouraging.
If it is giving, give generously.
If God has given you leadership ability,
take the responsibility seriously.
And if you have a gift for showing kindness to others,
do it gladly.*
Romans 12:6-8

A perceiver, server, teacher, motivator, giver, administrator, and empathizer . . . That's quite a list.

Which one are you?

Because everyone likes personality quizzes, we've created a short quiz to help pinpoint your gifts. Go through the questions and choose your best answer.

1. If you received a gift of $100, how would you use it?
   a. Put it in my savings for my dream trip
   b. Buy supplies to make my family a gourmet dinner
   c. Buy books
   d. Use it have a party for my friends

e. Give it to my favorite charity
f. Save it
g. Take a friend out to lunch

2. The house needs cleaning. What job would you do?
a. Choose to clean a room all by myself so I could be alone
b. Offer to clean the bathroom because I know no one else wants to do it
c. Show my friends the best way to paste wax the dining room table
d. Put on my favorite music and get everyone to dance while they cleaned
e. Bring over donuts and Starbucks for everyone
f. Make a list of to-dos and make assignments
g. Pinch-hit, helping whoever needs help or gets weary

3. You have been asked to participate in a charity event for the local women's shelter, identify the activity you would like to do:
a. Coordinate a prayer team to meet and pray for the event.
b. Coordinate the refreshments and make finger sandwiches.
c. Create and print flyers and distribute.
d. Agree to go to various churches and civic events and announce the event.
e. Make a contribution to the shelter to help with the expenses of the event.
f. Identify potential sponsors and call on them.
g. Talk with some of the women at the shelter and encourage them to share their story.

4. A good friend calls and shares a life crisis, how would you respond:
a. Pray with her on the phone and offer scripture of encouragement.
b. Volunteer to keep her pet or do her laundry.

c. Call several friends, explain the situation and organize a team to help the sister in crisis.
d. Call another friend and show up with her favorite coffee drink.
e. Send a beautiful floral arrangement with a gift card.
f. Ask specifics, analyze the situation, and offer a constructive solution to the problem.
g. Write a thoughtful note.

5. Your pastor makes an appeal for help with the children's Christmas program. What will you do?
a. Review the script and make suggestions for meaningful dialog.
b. Assist in making the costumes.
c. Contact the parents and remind them of rehearsal dates.
d. Announce the program in the worship services encouraging everyone to bring guests.
e. Collect contributions to help with the cost of props and costumes.
f. Search for clip art and create the program.
g. Collect, organize and place the necessary decorations.

6. You have 24 hours, just for you. Money is no object. How would you spend your day?
a. A day at the Spa all by yourself to read...soak...and relax.
b. Baking bread and cookies to stock the freezer for future Sister Circle meetings.
c. Organize your closet by color.
d. Call a group of friends, share snacks and play Mexican Train.
e. Volunteering at the local food bank after picking up donations.
f. A trip to your favorite museum or time at the library.
g. Shopping and lunch with favorite friends.

Add up your answers. Does one "letter" show up more than others? Or do you have a mix (most people have a mix to some degree).

Here is what your score says about your gift(s):
Mostly A's: You have the gift of Perceiving.
Mostly B's: You have the gift of Serving.
Mostly C's: You have the gift of Teaching.
Mostly D's: You have the gift of Motivating.
Mostly E's: You have the gift of Giving.
Mostly F's: You have the gift of Administration.
Mostly G's: You have the gift of Empathy.

To learn more, read our descriptions below and think about how the definitions relate to you.

• • •

• The Soul Sister (the Perceiver) •

The Soul Sister understands the larger picture and addresses the spiritual needs of those around her, keeping them centered on Christian principles. Although she sees sin in others, she also sees it in herself, and even rejoices in identifying her weaknesses, knowing that God will do a good work through her struggles. Because she *does* recognize her faults, she often has a poor self-image, always aware she can be a better person.

The Soul Sister is comfortable being alone. She recognizes that God is always present and finds companionship in Him. She holds herself to strict standards and desires to be obedient to God at all costs.

The Soul Sister is the "eyes" of the body. She sees what's truly going on and doesn't mince words, nor shy away from trying to persuade other people to see God at work around them.

Her Challenge:

The Soul Sister tends to be judgmental and blunt. She is so goal conscious that she forgets to praise others when they have a partial victory. She is pushy and intolerant of opinions she sees as anti-God. She needs to remember, "Patience can persuade a prince, and soft speech can break bones" Proverbs 25:15.

• • •

• The Server Sister (the Server) •

The Server Sister recognizes the needs of others and is quick to meet them. She dislikes clutter, is a detail person, and has a good memory. She enjoys people and will stay with a task until it is complete. She will do more than she's asked to do, but needs to feel appreciated. She does not want to lead, and would rather do a job herself than let someone else do it. The Server Sister has a hard time saying no and often ignores her own needs in order to help other people. She shows God's love through action.

The Server Sister is the "hands" of the body. She is the worker who's always there to help, addressing the practical needs of those around her.

Her Challenge:

The Server Sister may become pushy by being too eager to help, and doesn't understand when other people don't want to join in. She finds it hard to let others serve her and is easily hurt when she feels unappreciated. She needs to remember, "An offended friend is harder to win back than a fortified city" Proverbs 18:19.

• • •

• The Lister Sister (the Teacher) •

The Lister Sister likes things to be logical and based on truth. Facts are very important to her, and she loves to study and do research. She enjoys word studies and is skeptical of anything taken out of context. She is smart, sharp, and self-disciplined. She tries to keep her emotions under control and only has a select circle of friends. She has very strong convictions based on God's standards. She is often a crusader with a white horse, ready to ride.

The Lister Sister is the "mind" of the body, challenging the intellect of others, helping them learn.

Her Challenge:

The Lister Sister may get so caught up in facts that she neglects the practical life application of the truth. She may be legalistic and can get sidetracked by new projects that grab her interest. She doesn't like listening to other opinions and tends to be prideful about her own expertise and intelligence. She needs to remember, "Pride goes before destruction, and haughtiness before a fall" Proverbs 16:18.

• • •

• The Rah-Rah Sister (the Motivator) •

The Rah-Rah Sister loves life and people. She is a hands-on person, preferring to experience something rather than read about it. She is a good talker and a good listener who needs the give and take of a responsive audience. She doesn't judge others harshly but is accepting because she wants to help people be all they can be. She makes decisions easily and completes what she starts. She has lots of friends because she makes people feel good about themselves. She expects a lot from others and from herself.

The Rah-Rah Sister is the "mouth" of the body, sharing God's truth and nourishing the psychological side of her friends.

Her Challenge:

In her eagerness, the Rah-Rah Sister tends to interrupt to offer opinions or advice. She often has a cut-and-dried answer for everything and can be overly confident. Plus, if someone doesn't make an effort to change a problem in their lives, she gets perturbed and washes her hands of them. She needs to remember, "Those who control their tongue will have a long life; opening your mouth can ruin everything" Proverbs 13:3.

• • •

• The Giver Sister (the Giver) •

The Giver Sister gives freely of money, energy, time, possessions, and love. She gives the best she has to offer and gives toward a specific need. She is quick to volunteer. She is good at business and understands how to give wisely, making her a good steward of her resources. She realizes God is the source of her financial supply and as such feels special joy in giving, passing on what He has so generously provided.

The Giver Sister is the "arms" of the body. She extends her arms to give, making sure material needs are met.

Her Challenge:

The Giver Sister tends to pressure people to give and often wants control over how her gifts are used. She also can use financial giving as a way to get out of other responsibilities. She needs to remember, "The Lord's light penetrates the human spirit, exposing every hidden motive" Proverbs 20:27.

• • •

• The Fixer Sister (the Administrator) •

The Fixer Sister thrives on organization and is good at communicating and expressing her ideas. She's a leader with a broad perspective. She can get people to act, giving them a logical way to respond to a problem or task. Her enthusiasm comes from getting things done in the best, most efficient way possible. She respects authority, and doesn't need to get credit for her work as long as she feels satisfied. She is a list maker and a note writer. She likes to be challenged.

The Fixer Sister is the "shoulders" of the body, taking the responsibility others often don't want to assume. She takes care of functional needs, keeping people on track as she increases their vision towards God's purpose in their lives.

Her Challenge:

The Fixer Sister may get upset when others don't see her vision or don't work hard. She can be a perfectionist, expecting a lot from herself and everyone else. The "goal" is the thing, and this focus can often make her hard to deal with as she neglects the *people* involved in achieving that goal. She needs to remember that it is "Better to be patient than powerful; better to have self-control than to conquer a city" Proverbs 16:32.

• • •

• The Huggy Sister (the Empathizer) •

The Huggy Sister has a great capacity to love, always looks for the good in others, and is attracted to people who need her. She wants everyone to get along and takes great pains not to offend. She is trusting and trustworthy, but avoids confrontations and conflicts. She is thoughtful and is ruled by the heart rather than the head. She is cheerful and feels what others feel. She longs to love like God loves — unconditionally.

The Huggy Sister is the "heart" of the body, addressing the emotional needs of others. She feels *for* us and *with* us.

Her Challenge:

The Huggy Sister can be indecisive and easily hurt. Sometimes she empathizes too much and takes other people's pain and problems upon herself. She is often soft to the point of being wishy-washy, and it's hard for her to take a stand. She needs to remember, "The Lord is more pleased when we do what is right and just than when we offer Him sacrifices" Proverbs 21:3.

Q: Which Sister(s) do you identify with? Which Sister is nothing like you?

_____

_____

_____

_____

_____

_____

Heads up ladies! A caution to our competitive side. One gift is *not* better than another (sorry about that, Lister Sisters). Some abilities are flashy, some quiet. Some are more social, while others blossom behind the scenes. We repeat: one is not better than the other. All serve an essential part and purpose toward doing God's work. Speaking of . . . God, knowing our penchant for competition, addresses this:

• • •

God's Word Says:

"Yes, the body has many different parts, not just one part.
If the foot says, 'I am not a part of the body
because I am not a hand,'
that does not make it any less a part of the body.
And if the ear says, 'I am not part of the body
because I am not an eye,'
would that make it any less a part of the body?
If the whole body were an eye, how would you hear.
Or if your whole body were an ear,
how would you smell anything?
But our bodies have many parts,
He God put each part just where he wants it."
1 Corinthians 12:14-16

Just as he's put each part of our bodies just where He wants them, he's put *you* just where He wants *you*. The point is, dear sisters, we've been given *different* abilities in order to work *together* to get everything done — and done well! Appreciate each other, and be the best Soul, Server, Lister, Rah-Rah, Giver, Fixer, and Huggy Sister you can be!

Q: **Think of your close women friends. What Sister gift do they possess? How does that complement you? Or maybe frustrate you?**

_____

_____

_____

_____

_____

_____

_____

Now that you've thought about the abilities that God has handed out, we want to introduce you to the women from the Sister Circle novels because *they* are going to be the guinea pigs for the illustrations we use in this book. As you see these ladies in action, you may further identify and pinpoint your own gifts and abilities.

Another reason we've decided to use these fictional ladies in this way is to give you an "out." If you decide to discuss some of these sections with your sisters, you won't need to use each other as examples in the discussions, but can blast away at the fictional characters — at the traits you like, at the traits that drive you crazy. It's nice that way. Safe. Unlike the real-life sisters sitting with you, you don't have to see Audra at church, deal with Evelyn regarding the kid's carpool, or have lunch with Piper once a month. You can hate them, love them, and argue with them, but you *can't* offend them. So go for it.

Do you want to know a secret? The ladies living at the fictional Peerbaugh Place boarding house may not be real, but they are what *we* are: unpredictable, flawed, fabulous, and funny.

Let's meet them, and talk about them (instead of each other).

• • •

• Piper (a Perceiver/Soul Sister) •

In her mid-30s, Piper is more than ready to find the perfect someone.

Piper's ability to read people comes in handy in her role as a counselor at a high school, but she has a tendency to tell people what they don't want to hear. She likes to be around others, but she also finds herself good company. She has high standards — for others and herself.

She's a good daughter, a good friend, and a good sister to know.

• • •

• Summer (a Server/Server Sister) •

Summer is five years old and is totally comfortable being around adults. She's too smart and cute for her own good.

Summer loves to help, is eager to please, and often drives adults crazy as they try to keep her busy. She doesn't understand when other people don't want to help. She's a doer. A server.

If it weren't for her age, Summer would make someone a wonderful wife.

• • •

• Tessa (a Teacher/Lister Sister) •

Tessa is in her 70s. She's a bit prickly and likes things the way she likes them. She has all the answers and is very willing to share them with everyone.

Tessa is logical. Facts are very important, and she thrives on study and research. *However*, with all this information floating around in her brain, she can be a bit impatient with others less knowledgeable. She doesn't listen much and talks *too* much.

Is it any wonder Tessa has a select circle of friends?

• • •

• Mae (a Motivator/Rah-Rah Sister) •

Mae's an aging hippie. With her eccentric clothes, frizzy hair, and unique ways of doing things, you may not want her as a fashion consultant, but you would want her as a friend.

Mae loves life and can get people to do things they never expected. Give her an audience, and she's happy. But . . . whatever enters her brain comes out of her mouth.

Mae's frisky, a fabulous friend, and a frightful cook.

• • •

• Gillie (a Giver Sister) •

Gillie's divorce left her financially secure. She loves to give special presents to her friends (me! me! How about me?). Show her a cause, and she'll write you a check.

Gillie *could* be your fashion consultant and if you play her right, she might even buy you something.

• • •

• Audra (an Administrator/Fixer Sister) •

Audra is the single mother of Summer. She's never been married. Just out of college, she's starting a new life with her daughter. She's got guts, gumption, and goals.

Organization is the key to Audra's life. Give her a task, and she'll have a to-do list made in minutes, be ready to give assignments—and hold you accountable. Don't stand in her path when there's a job to be done or you might get recruited.

Unless your spices are neatly alphabetized, don't let Audra see inside your cupboards.

• • •

• Evelyn (an Empathizer/Huggy Sister) •

Evelyn is in her 50s and recently widowed. She has a great capacity to love. She always looks for the good in people and likes to be needed. She wants everyone at Peerbaugh Place to get along and takes great pains not to offend. She is a good friend but runs from a fuss. She is ruled by the heart rather than the head.

However, Evelyn can be indecisive because she wants people to like her. It's hard for her to take a stand. Hiding out on the porch is a favorite escape.

Evelyn likes to garden, hates to dust, and wears sensible shoes.

• • •

So, what do you think of these new friends? All of these women live in the Sister Circle novels.

Now that you've claimed one or more gifts, let's tackle the deep stuff. The first order of business is learning to deal with moods. Not that you've ever suffered any . . .

CHAPTER 2

• Moods •
(When Life's a Moody Mess)

"Search me, O God, and know my heart;
test me and know my anxious thoughts.
Point out anything in me that offends you,
and lead me along the path of everlasting life."
Psalm 139:23-24

• • •

It's mid-morning. The house is quiet and clean. The sun shines, a gentle breeze blows, the fragrance of fresh — and put away — laundry settles over you as you sit in your favorite chair, enjoying one more cup of coffee. The phone rings. It's the florist saying they have a delivery for you. Moments later your neighbor appears at your door with a home baked pie . . . just because. The flowers arrive with a sentimental note from your hubby.

Sure. Uh-huh.

The house is not clean, the dog has tracked in mud, the laundry is piled 3-feet high, and you're out of coffee. Your best friend calls and cancels lunch, the one you had on the calendar for weeks.

Although reality is less than perfect, we have no choice but to deal with it. Yet that doesn't mean we have to like it. That's where attitude comes in.

Good moods? We've got that down. Let's talk about the bad ones. So much of what influences our moods is not in our control, which only adds to our moodiness because no one likes being out of control. Yet when we allow our moods to take over, everything falls apart.

We can see it coming. From the moment we get up, everything that *can* go wrong does. Sleepy children, broken appliances, slow traffic, and cranky neighbors. The whole world can thank their lucky stars they aren't the telephone salesman who had the gall to offer us a super-duper deal to clean our carpets. Nasty reigns, and we like it that way. Life's a moody mess.

Let's join Evelyn as she gets herself worked up because everyone's forgotten her birthday.

Excerpt from *A Place to Belong*
Chapter 2

I'm old.

Evelyn pulled the dead geranium from its pot with extra vengeance. Out with the old, in with the new. She filled its place with a new, younger, prettier one and patted the soil around its roots. The new flower stood tall, strong on its stem, vibrant and very much alive. She gave it a *poing,* making it lose three red petals.

So there.

Evelyn set the newly planted pot on the porch railing, kicked a few sprinkles of dirt off the floor into the flower bed, took off her gardening gloves, and sat on the swing with an audible *"Oomph."*

This was pitiful. Couldn't she even bend down to pot a silly plant without having her muscles ache?

Obviously not. Especially not today when she was suddenly older than yesterday. She would never be fifty-eight again. *I'm being silly. I'm one day older than I was yesterday, not an entire year.*

Semantics.

She got the swing in motion and suddenly felt very alone. At breakfast no one had greeted her with shouts of "Happy birthday!" Piper, Lucinda, and Valerie had sipped their tea or coffee, eaten their oatmeal, and gone on with their lives as if today was like any other day. As the hours passed since then, the reality of their actions hit. And hit hard.

They forgot. Everyone forgot. She was alone.

She glanced at the empty space beside her. This was a swing meant for two. The lyrics to a Leslie Gore song intruded and Evelyn found herself singing "'It's My Party." Crying and parties. She let out a huff. "Nice pity party, Evelyn."

Q: When was the last time you had a pity party? (Did you have balloons and chocolate?)

_____

_____

_____

_____

_____

There's nothing wrong with throwing a pity party occasionally. But when we're in a mood, we need to figure out what brought it on. Don't wallow. Pin it down. Determine if the mood is worthy of the time and energy, then face it and move on. Life's too short — and pity-party decorations are too expensive.

How do we pinpoint the cause of our mood? Are we sick? hungry? tired? frustrated? angry? sad? Or is it something beyond _us_? If other people's actions are the cause of our moods, we have options: run, confront, talk, pout. Think ahead. Think of consequences. Figure out what works. But keep in mind, we can't usually change others, but we can change how we react to them, and we can choose whether we're going to let them get to us.

Then there are the moods that have been around awhile. Do they really need to be there? The God who created us knows our capacity for moods. We can't shock or discourage Him (thank goodness!). In fact, He provided us with PMS — a Positive Mood Solution. When our lives are controlled by the Holy Spirit, that includes our moods. God can handle it, which means we can, too. Through prayer. Through tuning into Him.

Remember we said that much of what affects our moods is out of our control. Guess what? God is in control of everything. Our earth isn't crashing into the stars, the oceans aren't drowning the land, and day and night happen pretty routinely. Oh yeah, and babies are born every day — which must mean God wants life to continue. Our moods are all about choosing a perspective-*ours* or *His*. That's where He can help. Talk to Him. Tell Him everything. Ultimately, He's the only one who can make a difference in our mood.

Some moods are meant to be shared. The Rah-Rah Sister is the perfect friend to call if you need to be pulled out of a mood (just be prepared for a straight answer to the problem!) Yet other sisters can help, too. This is where the true joy of sisterhood comes in. We implore you to find at least one sister to seek out at such times. Moods are inevitable but they *can* be managed. As Evelyn said, "So there."

Q: What moods are you most susceptible to?

_____

_____

_____

_____

_____

Q: Who suffers the most from your moods — and how?

_____

_____

_____

_____

_____

_____

Q: What could you do to get out of your moods sooner?

_____

_____

_____

_____

_____

_____

_____

Q: What woman friend could be your confidante?

_____

_____

_____

_____

_____

_____

• • •

Hunger and Thirst:

"Keep watch and pray, so that you will not give in to temptation.
For the spirit is willing, but the body is weak!"
Matthew 26:41

"If you need wisdom, ask our generous God,
and he will give it to you.
He will not rebuke you for asking. But when you ask him,
be sure that your faith is in God alone.
Do not waver, for a person with divided loyalty is as unsettled
as a wave of the sea that is blown and tossed by the wind.
Such people should not expect to receive anything from the Lord.
Their loyalty is divided between God and the world,
and they are unstable in everything they do."
James 1:5-8

"We can make our plans, but the Lord determines our steps."
Proverbs 16:9

• • •

For Me:

- Bake cookies.
- Color your hair — and help a friend do hers!
- Wave a flag. (Brenda put this in, Nancy has no idea what it means!)

For Others:

- Collect or make blankets for a city mission or women's safe home.
- Telephone a friend you haven't talked to in a long time.
- Send a card to someone — just because.

CHAPTER 3

• Intuition •
(Eyes in the Back of Your Head)

"Tune your ears to wisdom,
and concentrate on understanding.
Cry out for insight; and ask for understanding."
Proverbs 2:2-3

• • •

Women have a way of *knowing*. The value of women's intuition is undervalued in sitcoms, over-dramatized in many novels, and scoffed at by many a man. However, every woman knows there *are* those times you know that you know that you know. Right? Take Mae's intuition about Evelyn:

Excerpt from *An Undivided Heart*
Chapter 7

Mae leaned against the mantel. "How's Herb?"
"Fine."
"When was the last time you saw him?"
She wasn't sure. "Recently."
"This week?"
"Sure." She wasn't sure.
"Then you must have been in Chicago because Herb's been out of town visiting his son since Monday. I know. I went to Handy Hardware and they told me. He was getting back last night. Of course you knew that . . ."
Herb left town without telling her? "Of course I knew that." She moved on to the bookshelves.
Mae followed her like a plague in search of a victim.

"Sure you did."

"Mae . . ."

Mae took the dust cloth and spray away. "Look at me."

Evelyn had no choice.

"Now tell me the truth, sister to sister. Tell *yourself* the truth."

Evelyn shrugged.

"I'll take that shrug as an adamant yes. Admit it hurts to see the man you're interested in go on a date with someone else. Hurts bad."

"Don't be ridiculous."

Mae flicked a finger at the tip of her nose. "I promise not to be ridiculous if you promise not to be blind." She dropped the dusting equipment on a chair, took Evelyn's right hand, and raised it into the pledge position. "Promise?"

"Mae . . ."

"Promise?"

"Fine. Anything to get rid of you so I can finish my dusting."

Mae let go of Evelyn's hand and headed for the door. "Works for me. Ta-ta."

Evelyn stood in the parlor and watched her friend skip across the street. She hated when Mae was right.

And she was. She was.

Intuitive feelings do not evolve from nothing. They are influenced by our experiences as well as our personalities. For instance: When Brenda, a fair-weather West Coaster, came to visit Nancy, a hardy, unflappable Midwesterner, a tornado siren sounded. Nancy didn't look up. Brenda went into a panic mode, just certain she'd never see her grandchildren again.

When Nancy said, "Don't worry, it's nothing," Brenda said, "How do you know?" Without consulting the National Weather Service, Nancy replied. "I just know." Our intuitive reaction to this event was caused — and was based — on our experiences, and our personalities (plus, Nancy knew the siren was tested once a week at that particular time).

Q: Name a situation when you had a feeling about something without much concrete information. How did reality compare with your intuition?

_____

_____

_____

_____

_____

_____

_____

_____

_____

_____

Think of the last time you sat next to a stranger in a plane, at the pool, in an auditorium, or at church. Without making eye contact, could you sense a willingness — or unwillingness — to connect? Could you read each other without saying a word? Our female capacity to bond is based on intuition. If you sense a willingness to connect, then comes the choice: Do you open conversation and run the risk of getting involved in another person's life (possibly to a greater extent than you desire)? Or do you respond with nonverbal cues that you are unavailable?

Most of us can recall a time when we've felt trapped in a conversation. Perhaps we need to look at such a situation differently and turn it from a burden to an opportunity to help someone who needs to talk.

Are you a Soul Sister? Or a Huggy Sister? If so, you might be the kind of sister who listens well. Yet you offer different things in return. The Soul Sister often has good insight into the spiritual needs of her sisters, while the Huggy Sister offers compassion. In either case, ask the Holy Spirit to give you wisdom and sensitivity as you share your gift.

God loves a good listener.

Q: Name a time you listened to a stranger. Did you express genuine compassion or simply endure it? What was the person's reaction?

_____

_____

_____

_____

_____

_____

_____

_____

_____

Q: Tell about a time you needed to talk to a stranger and they listened. How did it make you feel?

_____

_____

_____

_____

_____

_____

_____

_____

_____

Situation: Your husband, child, or roommate comes home from work. You take one look and say, "What's wrong?"

"Nothing."

"I don't buy it. What's wrong?"

This is the perfect example of women's intuition. You sense the emotion even before it's expressed. Yet when the person tells you it's nothing, what do you do? What _can_ you do? What _should_ you do? Do you really need to know all the details? Upset is upset.

You probably can't fix it anyway. Think before you overreact and take the non-responsiveness as an insult to your very being. (Been there/done that.)

Q: What can you do to accept "nothing" as the final answer to "what's wrong"? (We know it's hard.)

_____

_____

_____

_____

_____

_____

_____

As mysterious as it sounds, intuition is often based on logic, deductive reasoning, and experience. For instance, we use our intuition to protect and nurture our family. If our daughter brings home a friend who makes our bells clang, it's our God-given responsibility to act on that warning and speak out when the time is right. At the risk of being wrong, we need to listen to our instincts. What did our mothers say? *Better safe than sorry.*

The intuition of a woman who has faith in Christ is fueled and directed by God, which can be a great and essential weapon of protection against the evil of the world. Those gentle (and sometimes not so gentle) nudges that warn us of potential harm need to be acted upon. God has not given us the gift of intuition to be ignored.

God gave men muscles so they can protect their families from physical harm. God gave women intuition to guard the hearts, minds, and souls of their family. God covered all the bases, and even supplied the details.

• • •

God's Word Says:

"Therefore, put on every piece of God's armor
so you will be able to resist the enemy in the time of evil.
Then after the battle you will still be standing firm.
*Stand your ground, putting on the **belt** of truth*
*and the **body armor** of God's righteousness.*
For shoes, put on the peace that comes from the Good News
so that you will be fully prepared.
*In addition to all of these, hold up the **shield** of faith*
to stop the fiery arrows of the devil.
*Put on salvation as your **helmet**,*
*and take the **sword** of the Spirit, which is the word of God.*
Pray in the Spirit at all times and on every occasion.
Stay alert and be persistent in your prayers
for all believers everywhere."
Ephesians 6:13-18

Q: **What part of your armor is weak? (What can you do to make it strong?)**

_____

_____

_____

_____

_____

_____

• • •

Hunger and Thirst:

"For God speaks again and again,
though people do not recognize it.
He speaks in dreams, in visions of the night
when deep sleep falls on people as they lie in their beds.
He whispers in their ears and terrifies them with warnings.
He makes them turn from doing wrong;
he keeps them from pride."
Job 33:14-17

"My father taught me, 'Take my words to heart.
Follow my commands
and you will live. Get wisdom, develop good judgment.
Don't forget my words or turn away from them.
Don't turn your back on wisdom, for she will protect you.
Love her, and she will guard you.
Getting wisdom is the wisest thing you can do!
And whatever else you do, develop good judgment.
If you prize wisdom, she will make you great.
Embrace her, and she will honor you.
She will place a lovely wreath on your head;
she will present you with a beautiful crown.' "
Proverbs 4:4-9

"Oh, how great are God's riches and wisdom and knowledge!
How impossible it is for us
to understand his decisions and his ways!
For who can know the Lord's thoughts?
Who knows enough to give him advice?
And who has given him so much that he needs to pay it back?
For everything comes from him and exists by his power
and is intended for his glory.
All glory to him forever! Amen."
Romans 11:36

"So be careful how you live.
Don't live like fools, but like those who are wise.
Make the most of every opportunity in these evil days.
Don't act thoughtlessly,
but understand what the Lord wants you to do.
Don't be drunk with wine, because that will ruin your life.
Instead, be filled with the Holy Spirit,
singing psalms and hymns and spiritual songs among yourselves,
and making music to the Lord in your hearts.
And give thanks for everything to God the Father
in the name of our Lord Jesus Christ."
Ephesians 5:15-20

*"The Lord keeps you from all harm and watches over your life.
The Lord keeps watch over you as you come and go,
both now and forever."*
Psalm 121:7-8

• • •

For Me:

- Go to the library and study something, or access an online course.
- Pray for each family member.
- Buy new jammies. Cute frilly ones.

For Others:

- Offer to take an elderly person on errands.
- Think of someone who might need something and make it happen.
- Bring dinner to a shut-in.

CHAPTER 4

• Self-Sufficiency •
(No, You Can't Do It Yourself!)

*"For I can do everything through Christ,
who gives me strength."*
Philippians 4:13

• • •

All together now: Burn your bra, put on those hip-huggers, rake the shag carpet, and sing, *"I am woman, hear me roar. . ."*
Yuck.
That song was the anthem of women's lib in the 1970's. It was a time we were told we could do anything. We were supposed to be independent and self-sufficient. We were supposed to like polyester, and roaring was supposed to make us feel strong.
Pardon our rebellion, but the pictures we have of ourselves in double-knit make us cringe, and roaring only makes us hoarse.
Being self-sufficient is a good thing. It feels good. We feel capable, and it feeds our ego.
We brought up our kids in the independent tradition. When our children first said, "I can do it myself!" we applauded. We cheered when they took their first step, tied their own shoes, or drove themselves to school (no more carpool lane!) Why is it that those childhood expressions of independence and self-sufficiency make us proud, but when we face a situation like the empty nest, we pray our kids don't forget where we live? Insecurity knows no age limit.
In the scene below, Mae is the mother of independent

children. She knows why they didn't show up for Mother's Day, but that doesn't make it any easier:

Excerpt from *The Sister Circle*
Chapter 12

Mae lay in bed, very much awake. Everyone else was with their respective families, celebrating Mother's Day.

But it was just another day for her.

She couldn't remember the last time she'd gotten any special attention on Mother's Day. Five years ago? Ten? *And whose fault is that?*

Mae subjected her pillow to a stranglehold. She loved her children. But did they love her?

If they loved me they'd call me on Mother's Day. They'd send me a card, they'd —

They can't send me a card if they don't know where I live. What was the last address I shared with them?

She couldn't remember. Her self-imposed freedom, instead of offering wide open vistas, suddenly seemed very closed — with very high walls.

A prison of loneliness.

Mae pulled the covers over her head.

Mae's situation might be extreme, yet the attitude of "I don't need you" is the hurtful part of independence. We want our loved ones to have a healthy dose of independence, yet also yearn for them to want us around. Being too self-sufficient creates a prison of loneliness that has strong bars and doors that are hard to unlock.

Nancy has a self-sufficient friend who had minor surgery. Stuck at home a few days, no one came to visit, no one sent flowers. No one brought meals. There were a few phone calls, but no real attention. She was hurt. Afterward, she shared her hurt, and her friends were shocked by her reaction. They assumed since she was such a capable, independent woman she didn't need — or even want — such attention. They assumed she had it under control. But she didn't.

Q: Who have you chased off by being a self-sufficient, capable woman?

_____

_____

_____

_____

_____

A tip: When you recognize you are not totally self-sufficient and are a little over-whelmed, your Server Sister or Huggy Sister friends are the perfect people to call. They're probably just aching for a chance to help, or meet you at the mall to shop or do lunch. They'll give you the encouragement you need. Just ask.

Q: What self-sufficient woman do you know who might need a little special attention?

_____

_____

_____

_____

_____

Let's face it. We try to be self-sufficient in all areas of our lives. Physically, we like to take care of our health and our bodies. Emotionally, we don't want to be considered a cry baby or weak. Intellectually, we like to be in-the-know in regard to our finances and the world. Spiritually, we want to know God's there, but are proud we can handle things pretty well on our own. Nowadays, nobody we know longs to play the dependent _femme fatale_ role.

So where's the balance? The only way to find it is to admit and develop our ultimate dependence on God. Give it up, sisters. We aren't in control, He is. Acknowledging the true source of our strength doesn't make us weak, it makes us whole. Dependence on Him frees us from having to solve every problem and takes worry far, far away.

Q: Be creative. Every day come up with ways to remind yourself to depend on God. Keeping a list helps.

_____
_____
_____
_____
_____
_____
_____
_____
_____

• • •

Hunger and Thirst:

"I give you thanks, O Lord, with all my heart;
I will sing your praises before the gods.
I bow before your holy Temple as I worship.
I praise your name for your unfailing love and faithfulness;
for your promises are backed by all the honor of your name.
As soon as I pray, you answer me;
you encourage me by giving me strength."
Psalm 138:1-3

"Because of the privilege and authority God has given me,
I give each of you this warning:
Don't think you are better than you really are.
Be honest in your evaluation of yourselves,
measuring yourselves by the faith God has given us.
Just as our bodies have many parts
and each part has a special function, so it is with Christ's body.
We are many parts of one body, and we all belong to each other."
Romans 12:3-5

"For I can do everything
through Christ, who gives me strength."
Philippians 4:13

46

"A person standing alone can be attacked and defeated,
but two can stand back-to-back and conquer.
Three are even better, for a triple-braided cord is not easily broken."
Ecclesiastes 4:12

• • •

For Me:

- Have a girls' night out.
- Exchange babysitting (or dog sitting) duties.
- Buy a magazine you've never bought before. And read it all the way through.

For Others:

- Take a goodie bag or gift card to a friend who needs encouragement.
- Have a garage sale and give proceeds to charity.
- Collect hotel toiletries for a rescue mission.

CHAPTER 5

• Loneliness and Solitude •
(No Woman Is an Island)

"I can never escape from your Spirit!
I can never get away from your presence!
If I go up to heaven, you are there;
if I go down to the grave, you are there.
If I ride the wings of the morning,
if I dwell by the farthest oceans,
even there your hand will guide me,
and your strength will support me."
Psalm 139:7-10

• • •

Have you ever stood in a crowded shopping mall with people brushing by on every side, and suddenly your mind and heart are flooded with the feeling that you are all alone, separate from the rest of the world?

Me neither.

Seriously, loneliness has little to do with the number of people around you. It's all about the lack of soul bonding with soul, mind bonding with mind, emotion bonding with emotion.

Our leading character, Evelyn Peerbaugh, has just suffered the death of her husband. Her finances are in dire straits:

Excerpt from *The Sister Circle*
Chapter 1

The silence became a vacuum that sucked away all her energy. She let the solidity of the door guide her as she slid to the floor. Her challis skirt got hung up on a knee, revealing her slip. She moved to pull it primly down, but when she realized there was no one around to see, let it be. That would take getting used to, having no one around.

The tears began to flow uncontrollably — sobs she never expected. Thoughts of her life began to unfold like a book being opened . . . She'd lived a pleasant, respectable life, enjoyed good friends, and reared an independent son. Now, in her golden years, was this all she had to show for it? Decades of humdrum, monotonous existence coupled with financial struggle?

With effort, she took a deep breath, but the air entered in ragged pieces. Why did she feel so worn out? She used to be full of energy, and yet now, as a widow, her strength vacillated between the frenzy of a worker ant and a bug squashed beneath someone's foot.

As if sensing her mood, Peppers nudged her face into Evelyn's calf. Evelyn picked her up and let the Calico find her favorite position on Evelyn's shoulder; like a baby going to be burped. Peppers' purring resonated against Evelyn's chest like the comforting sound of cicadas on a summer evening.

She sniffed loudly and used her skirt to wipe her face. Then, without warning, she spoke aloud, "God, if You're out there . . . help! Tell me what I'm supposed to do next."

Q: Identify the last time you were truly lonely.

_____

_____

_____

_____

_____

_____

_____

Loneliness doesn't need to overwhelm us. With God's help we can learn to put it in proper perspective as a mood and not a permanent state of mind. Recognize it and accept it as a normal part of life.

How? Take a break: Walk outside or take a walk with a friend. Do an act of kindness for someone to take your mind off yourself. Or in a busy place, make eye contact with one person and strike up a conversation. Even a few moments of chit-chat can take our loneliness outside ourselves where it has a chance to dissipate.

Some sisterly advice: The best friendships are the ones that nurture our soul. Sisters of faith have a way of knowing when they can come alongside us in our loneliness or step back when we need solitude. Cultivate "faith friendships."

Jesus said: "This is my commandment: Love each other in the same way I have loved you. There is no greater love than to lay down one's life for one's friends" (John 15: 12-13). Be there for each other.

If you are a Lister Sister, know that you have a special ability to influence others with the truth of God's Word. Use your gift to help a lonely sister realize she is never really alone and God may want to use her loneliness to impart special insights into her heart. Making someone feel special in Christ is a sure antidote to loneliness.

If we define loneliness as a lack of bonding with others, solitude is the choice to bond with ourselves. Selected silence can keep us sane. Being alone with quiet thoughts, creative ideas, meditative moments, can enrich us as much as a piece of chocolate or crusty French bread with lots of butter (okay, who's hungry?) Too often we hurry to *fill* every lonely moment yet God might be trying to use those moments to speak to us.

• • •

God's Word Says:

"Be still, and know that I am God!"
Psalm 46:10

Q: Where do you — could you — find solitude?

_____

_____

_____

_____

_____

_____

Where did Jesus go to recharge? He didn't seek out the crowds, nor stop living. When He could, He withdrew into solitude — to pray. He was never alone, and neither are we. God is with us in every circumstance, in every moment, in any mood. He can be the Savior in our solitude. In fact, He instructs us to be still. Stop fighting it. Be still. And find the peace that comes through knowing Him better.

• • •

Hunger and Thirst:

_"'For I know the plans I have for you,' says the Lord.
'They are plans for good and not for disaster,
to give you a future and a hope.
In those days when you pray, I will listen.
If you look for me wholeheartedly, you will find me.
I will be found by you,' says the Lord.
'I will end your captivity and restore your fortunes.
I will gather you out of the nations where I sent you
and will bring you home again to your own land.' "_
Jeremiah 29:11-14

_"Don't worry about anything; instead, pray about everything.
Tell God what you need, and thank him for all he has done.
Then you will experience God's peace,
which exceeds anything we can understand.
His peace will guard your hearts and minds
as you live in Christ Jesus."_
Philippians 4:6-7

"Be still in the presence of the Lord,
and wait patiently for him to act."
Psalm 37:7

"Faith is the confidence that what we hope for will actually happen;
it gives us assurance about things we cannot see.
Through their faith, the people in days of old
earned a good reputation."
Hebrews 11:1-2

• • •

For Me:
- Sit in a church sanctuary in the middle of the day. *Hello, God, it's me . . .*
- Take a walk. Breathe deeply. Really look around — and inside.
- Light some candles and enjoy a bubble bath.

For Others:
- Call your church or a local retirement home and get the names of people who might like a visit.
- Go out for coffee with a friend and let her do most of the talking.
- Pray for one specific friend, asking God how you could be a blessing in her life.

CHAPTER 6

• Waiting •
(Tapping Into Patience. Now!)

"But those who trust in the Lord will find new strength.
They will soar high on wings like eagles.
They will run and not grow weary. They will walk and not faint."
Isaiah 40:31

• • •

Oh, to be a child with no concept of time. We hate to wait. At the doctor's office, in traffic, at the grocery store. Don't tell us you've never hurried toward the checkout to get in front of the lady who's pushing a full shopping cart. We even get impatient waiting for the microwave to ding. Our culture breeds instant gratification.

There are two kinds of waiting. *Real-time* waiting— waiting for the movie that starts in 20 minutes. Or *open-ended* waiting. Here's Piper dealing with an open-ended wait in her life:

Excerpt from *An Undivided Heart*
Chapter 1

Piper felt Mae's eyes on her and wished she could deflect some of the sister radar.

It didn't work.

"Have you seen your handsome doctor lately?"

Bingo.

"He's not my handsome doctor."

"Which is the real problem before us this evening, isn't it?"

Piper downed her milk so she'd have a reason to get up from the table, pretending to want more. "The book's closed on Gregory and me. You know that, Mae."

"Zounds, sister. I see pages turning, practically flapping in the wind, trying to get to the next chapter."

Piper leaned against the refrigerator. "You're reading way ahead."

"But if he does get with the program . . ."

Piper had to laugh. "I've never heard that phrase used in conjunction with becoming a Christian."

"An oversight, I'm sure." Mae patted Piper's place at the table. "Sit down and tell Auntie Mae all about it."

Piper returned to her seat. "There's nothing to tell."

"Gracious Gobstoppers, Pipe, you still love him. That's plenty to tell."

"I keep praying God will take the feeling away."

"Why? Love's a good thing."

"Not when it can never be fulfilled."

"Never tell God never. Maybe He's working on Gregory's heart this very minute."

Piper shrugged.

Why is the Open-Ended Wait so difficult? Because it's out of our control, *and* there is the chance that what we hope for might never come about. That's scary. We like to know what's going to happen — and when.

But remember this: God is never late and never early. The issues that involve open-ended waiting are usually large in scope. Life issues. Important stuff. It helps to remember that God has a plan, and He is in control. Waiting is part of that plan.

Think about planting a seed. Every seed needs to be planted at a certain depth, in a certain season. The gestation time — the waiting time — is different for each one. The root system and everything that is needed for that plant to grow and thrive is being developed out of sight — in its own time. God plants seeds in our heart for companionship, family, purpose, and career. He plants them at a prescribed depth, known only to Him. At the right time — if no one digs us up too early, if we don't force ourselves out too soon — we will bloom and grow and be all that He intends us to be. We need to allow ourselves to bloom where we're planted.

So while we're waiting for God's plan to be fulfilled, we need to remind ourselves that the plan is bigger than us.

Sometimes we're waiting on other people, sometimes we're waiting for circumstances to be just right, and sometimes God is waiting — on us. As the Creator of time, He's got all the time in the world to wait for us to get with His program. He is incredibly patient. We can do things *our* way in *our* time, or do things the *right* way, in *God's* time.

Think about it.

Q: What open-ended issue are you waiting on?

_____

_____

_____

_____

_____

_____

_____

_____

_____

_____

Q: What has to fall into place before you get an answer?

_____

_____

_____

_____

_____

_____

_____

_____

_____

_____

Q: How could it be that God is waiting on you?

_____

_____

_____

_____

_____

_____

The last issue in regard to waiting involves how we use our time during the waiting process. Are we constructive or brooding? Is it possible to view waiting as a good thing and embrace it with anticipation?

• • •

God's Word Says:

"For everything there is a season,
a time for every activity under heaven.
A time to be born and a time to die.
A time to plant and a time to harvest.
A time to kill and a time to heal.
A time to tear down and a time to build up.
A time to cry and a time to laugh.
A time to grieve and a time to dance.
A time to scatter stones and a time to gather stones.
A time to embrace and a time to turn away.
A time to search and a time to quit searching.
A time to keep and a time to throw away.
A time to tear and a time to mend.
A time to be quiet and a time to speak.
A time to love and a time to hate.
A time for war and a time for peace."
Ecclesiastes 3: 1-8

Think about waiting in line an hour to go on a ride at an amusement park. Remember seeing signs that say "30-minute wait from this point"? Do we turn around and leave? No. We wait because the reward ahead — the three-minutes of screaming and laughter — is worth the wait.

Unfortunately, God doesn't provide us with signs saying how long it's going to be.

Or does He?

If we look close enough we will probably see evidence He is at work during our wait. Knowing that, shouldn't we embrace the idea of waiting with expectation?

Remember those moods we talked about? If we approach waiting in a woe-is-me mode, we could miss a blessing. But if we turn it around and wait with expectation, there can be joy *in* the waiting. His will is worth the wait.

· · ·

Hunger and Thirst:

"Then the Lord said to me, 'Write my answer plainly on tablets,
so that a runner can carry the correct message to others.
This vision is for a future time.
It describes the end, and it will be fulfilled.
If it seems slow in coming, wait patiently,
for it will surely take place. It will not be delayed.' "
Habakkuk 2:2-3

"I waited patiently for the Lord to help me,
and he turned to me and heard my cry.
He lifted me out of the pit of despair, out of the mud and the mire.
He set my feet on solid ground and steadied me as I walked along.
He has given me a new song to sing,
a hymn of praise to our God.
Many will see what he has done and be amazed.
They will put their trust in the Lord."
Psalm 40:1-3

"Let us hold tightly without wavering to the hope we affirm,
for God can be trusted to keep his promise. Let us think of ways to
motivate one another to acts of love and good works."
Hebrews 10:23-24

"Therefore, since we are surrounded by such a huge crowd
of witnesses to the life of faith,
let us strip off every weight that slows us down,
especially the sin that so easily trips us up.
And let us run with endurance the race that God has set before us."
Hebrews 12:1

"Keep on asking, and you will receive what you ask for.
Keep on seeking, and you will find.
Keep on knocking, and the door will be opened to you."
Matthew 7:7

• • •

For Me:
- Visit a peaceful place that brings you comfort.
- Think of some short-term thing you've been waiting to do — and do it.
- Get in the longest line, and have a nice chat with your fellow wait-ers. Enjoy the wait!

For Others:
- Visit a retirement home or hospital.
- Donate professional outfits to organizations that assist women in re-entering the work force.
- Help serve at a soup kitchen.

CHAPTER 7

• Gossip •
(An Accident Waiting to Happen)

"A troublemaker plants seeds of strife;
gossip separates the best of friends."
Proverbs 16:28

• • •

You would never intentionally jump into "gossip gab." Would you?

Soap operas depict women as cruel, intentional gossips, but we know we are not one of *those* women.

Absolutely not . . . Maybe?

Okay, sometimes.

There are so many variations of gossip, it's surprising some writer hasn't written a book on *Creative Ways to Gossip Without Guilt.*

But alas, it's not to be. Gossip is an accident waiting to happen, and it does make us feel guilty — or at least it should.

Gossip isn't usually planned. If often happens by accident with casualties guaranteed.

Just as we don't get into our cars planning to crash (yet we fasten our seatbelts before leaving the driveway, just in case), we need to be smart sisters and create a few "safety belts" to protect us from gossip because gossip (often disguised as chit-chat) may cause more than just bruised feelings or fractured friendships. It can cause a major emotional casualty.

You know how it happens. You're in the middle of a conversation and all of a sudden you realize a head-on collision is imminent. The name of a person or an incident is mentioned and before you know it someone leans close and says those enticing, seductive words "Did you know . . . ?"

If you want to play the role of a reporter for the Gabby Times Gazette, you can require source documents for all the juicy information in an attempt to make yourself appear logical, unbiased, and certainly not as bad as those who are obviously getting a great deal of pleasure out of the sordid details. But that would be a mere act, a token of rationalization, giving ourselves permission to listen. We know our true motives. We listen because it makes us feel good. Feel superior.

In the following scene, Mae probably wishes her husband had not been home when she had the perfect opportunity to share some juicy information with a friend. But the truth is, God was probably protecting her from herself.

Excerpt from *'Round the Corner*
Chapter 8

Collier Ames fingered the handle of his mug of tea. "Now, now, Mae. Don't go jumping to any delusions."

Mae paced in front of the kitchen sink. "It's *conclusions*, and I'm not jumping. It's standing smack-dab in front of me waving a hand in front of my face. Gracious gophers, Collie, she was standing in front of me, plain as day."

"Lots of people have a second job."

"Maybe. But why has she never said anything? From what I've seen and heard, Gail makes a big deal about being some executive at Lanigan Marketing. She's even put Heddy down for *her* job as the hostess at Ruby's."

Collier took a sip of tea. "Maybe she likes the food at Burger Madness? They do have a super pork tenderloin."

"Oh, puh-leeze. Next you'll be saying she took the job so she could wear the spiffy uniform."

He shrugged.

Men. Mae stopped pacing and tapped her lips. "I've got to go tell Evelyn."

"Oh no you don't."

She grabbed her coat. "Oh yes, I do. It's my duty as her friend."

Collier got up and took Mae's coat from her. He hung it up on the hook by the back door. "Since you don't know the facts behind Gail's job, I suggest you remain quiet. There's got to be a reasonable explanation."

"Not necessarily."

"Yes, necessarily. Gail's not working at a burger place in a town thirty minutes away, for the fun of it."

"Then I have to know why."

"You don't have to know why. It's none of your business, Mae."

"But Evelyn's my friend and she's being conned."

He made a face. "How so?"

"She's rented a room to a con artist. Gail's pretended to be something she's not."

Collier nodded and riddled his fingers on the table. "Let me ask you this: As far as you know, has Gail paid her rent in full?"

"As far as I know."

"Has she brandished any firearms, carried out any drug deals, or been seen entertaining any shady characters on the porch of Peerbaugh Place?"

Mae dug her fists into her hips. "Collie."

"I rest my case. Leave it alone, Mae. If Gail is lying, she must have a good reason. The truth will come out eventually. It always does."

Mae felt a pout coming on. He was right, but Mae never found any fun in that. Or in waiting.

Go ahead, you can pout along with Mae. But be aware that those caution signs and detours (like husbands overhearing a phone conversation) help us avoid accidents. Try to see them as a blessing.

Expressing concern, giving constructive criticism, and offering helpful advice are frequently used as excuses for getting involved in a conversation about a third party. However, here is a good rule you can fasten around your loose lips as tightly as you fasten your seatbelt: if you can't say what you have to say to a person's face, don't say it!

We have a challenge for you: Be a brave Sister. Make us proud of our sisterhood, and be the one to stop the gossip accident from leaving casualties in your circle. This is going to take courage, and yes, you may even run the risk of being labeled "Miss Goody Two Shoes," but wear those shoes proudly and polish them often.

One alternative is to walk away from such a conversation, but let's go one step further. When you witness a discussion that's headed for a crash, have the courage to prevent the accident. Stop the gossip. Cold. Put up a roadblock, sound the sirens, and pull the conversation over to the side of the road. A line as simple as, "You know what? We shouldn't talk about her like this," or "that's *not* what I know to be true about her," might be enough. Try it. You may be surprised how good it feels when you take that brave step.

Q: Do you know someone who is a gossip? *Don't answer.*

Q: What was the last juicy bit of gossip you heard? *Don't answer.*

Do you get the point? Please shut your pretty mouth. Loose lips sink ships — and friendships.

Q: Create two or three "exit" lines from gossip (be more creative than we were). Write them here. Then memorize these lines and accident-proof your conversations!

_____

_____

_____

_____

_____

• • •

God's Word Says:

"There will be no mercy for those
who have not shown mercy to others.
But if you have been merciful, God will be merciful when he judges."
James 2:13

And here's a concept: Show mercy to the gossip victim. If you've heard talk, put yourself in the high heels of the target. Jesus said, "Love each other. Just as I have loved you, you should love each other. Your love for one another will prove to the world that you are my disciples" (John 13:34-35). Showing some sisterly love and compassion to the woman who's being verbally pounced upon will make you feel great because it's the right thing to do (you know it is). Plus, it might dispel future gossip.

Gossip, as with so many other aspects of sisterhood, comes down to the Golden Rule: Do unto others as you would have them do unto you.

Case closed. Lips locked. Your integrity intact.

Q: How would you feel if you knew you were the victim of gossip? (or have you been?)

_____

_____

_____

_____

_____

_____

_____

_____

Q: If someone knew some juicy gossip about you, what would you hope they'd do? How would you deal with them?

_____

_____

_____

_____

_____

_____

• • •

Hunger and Thirst:

"Await the mercy of our Lord Jesus Christ,
who will bring you eternal life.
In this way, you will keep yourselves safe in God's love.
And you must show mercy to those whose faith is wavering.
Rescue others by snatching them from the flames of judgment.
Show mercy to still others, but do so with great caution,
hating the sins that contaminate their lives."
Jude 21-23

"A gossip goes around telling secrets,
so don't hang around with chatterers."
Proverbs 20:19

"As surely as a north wind brings rain,
so a gossiping tongue causes anger!"
Proverbs 25:23

"And so blessing and cursing come pouring out of the same mouth.
Surely, my brothers and sisters, this is not right!
Does a spring of water bubble out
with both fresh water and bitter water?
Does a fig tree produce olives, or a grapevine produce figs?
No, and you can't draw fresh water from a salty spring."
James 3:10-12

• • •

For Me:
- Try a new shade of lipstick.
- Smile at a stranger.
- Say "Bless you" to a store clerk.

For Others:
- Have a "You are Special" party. Draw names and bring a small gift to a fellow sister, along with a note telling her how special she is.

- Say thank you to someone you don't know.
- If you've hurt someone by gossiping, apologize. Make things right!

CHAPTER 8

• Sexuality •
(Being Real)

"Create in me a clean heart, O God.
Renew a loyal spirit within me."
Psalm 51:10

• • •

Ha. Fooled ya. This section isn't really about sexuality, but we knew you'd never turn here if we used the real title: MORALITY. Don't you dare turn the page (Big Sister is watching!) But just to appease you, we'll give you an excerpt that has a bit of spice in it:

Excerpt from *'Round the Corner*
Chapter 3

A man had Heddy pressed against the counter—and against each other—kissing. Hard.

Evelyn hadn't meant to gasp, but she must have because Heddy's eyes shot open and looked at her over the man's shoulder. She pushed the man away. "Oh."

The man turned around. "Oh, hello."

"Hello," Evelyn said.

Heddy brushed a hand over her mouth, then let it run through her hair. "Did we wake you?"

"I couldn't sleep. I came down for a glass of milk."

Heddy stepped away from the man. "We were just..." She scanned the counter. "Going to have some cake. Would that be all right? I see you've baked. We could smell it when we came in. What kind—?"

Nice try. "Are you going to introduce us?" Evelyn

asked.

"Of course. Evelyn this is Bill—"

"Bob," the man said, extending his hand. "Bob Olson."

A sickly puce color swept over Heddy's skin. "Bob, this is Evelyn Peerbaugh, the proprietress of this establishment."

Evelyn shook his hand, wanting him gone—wanting to be gone herself. She was embarrassed for Heddy, yet incensed that she'd been drawn in to witness such a thing. To kiss a man and not know his name? What kind of woman was Heddy?

Heddy took Bob's hand and pulled him toward the door. "I think we'd better call it a night."

"Sure, sure. Night, Evelyn."

They left Evelyn alone in the kitchen. She wished there was a back stairway she could take to her room. If only she hadn't heard the giggling; hadn't been curious. Now, what was she supposed to do? She didn't want to put herself in the position of being house-mother to her tenants and yet—

Heddy returned but only took a single step into the room. "I wish you hadn't seen that."

"Me too."

"I really did know his name."

"Not well enough."

If Evelyn had not appeared in the kitchen and discovered Heddy with her male friend, she would not have had to deal with the reality of Heddy's behavior. What we refuse to acknowledge we don't have to deal with, right? Ignorance can be bliss. Or not.

Who are we fooling? Ignoring the situation doesn't make it go away. Face it, sisters, in the midst of such a moral dilemma, you have to make a decision. Will it be based on *preferences* or *principles?*

Issues such as when, where, and how we worship is a *preference*. Organ music or electric guitar? Shorts or suits? Pure preference. Dyed hair or natural? A preference. Eating dinner at five or eight? A preference.

Sometimes things happen that aren't that important. We can ignore them and walk away. Yet when it does matter, it's time to take a stand.

The Ten Commandments are principles that are given to us in the form of a *command*, not a suggestion.

• • •

The Ten Commandments

1. *God is God.*
2. *Worship the true God.*
3. *Don't misuse God's name.*
4. *Have a day of rest.*
5. *Honor your parents.*
6. *Do not murder.*
7. *Do not commit adultery.*
8. *Do not steal.*
9. *Do not lie.*
10. *Do not covet.*

We often spend too much time trying to persuade others to adapt to our preferences when we should spend our energy taking a stand for our principles. Don't sweat the small stuff, but still remember it's *not* all small stuff.

So how do we take a stand while respecting the rights and feelings of others? It's tough, because though we can influence another person's behavior, we can't easily alter their belief system. You can prevent your 8-year-old son from stealing a pack of gum at the grocery store by standing close by and watching, but when your back is turned, he still might steal because *his* principles are in charge. As a parent you have a chance to influence your children's principles, but there will come a time . . .

Character is who you are when no one's looking. The question is: Are you going to *be* a character or have character? Morality is a choice. Here's a quote from Nancy: *Characters live to be noticed; people with character notice how they live.*

Which one are you?

Q: Thinking of acquaintances (without naming names), what's a choice you've witnessed that you don't agree with?

_____
_____
_____
_____
_____
_____
_____
_____

Q: How did you react?

_____
_____
_____
_____
_____
_____
_____

Q: By changing your reaction, could you get a better response from them or within yourself?

_____
_____
_____
_____
_____

As far as reacting to other people . . . you Lister and Fixer Sisters out there? The challenge to your gifts is that you can get so caught up in facts that you forget to use your heart. Borrow a bit from the Huggy Sister and react with your heart as well as your head. Both have their place. And their time to shine.

Above all, no matter what sister trait you hold, be an example. Our own well-lived lives are the best way of standing up to an immoral world. The best way to become an example is to study the Word. As St. Francis of Assisi said, "Preach the gospel. If necessary, use words."

• • •

Hunger and Thirst:

"A sensible person wins admiration,
but a warped mind is despised."
Proverbs 12:8

"And the Holy Spirit helps us in our weakness.
For example, we don't know what God wants us to pray for.
But the Holy Spirit prays for us with groanings
that cannot be expressed in words.
And the Father who knows all hearts
knows what the Spirit is saying,
for the Spirit pleads for us believers
in harmony with God's own will.
And we know that God causes everything to work together
for the good of those who love God
and are called according to his purpose for them."
Romans 8:26-28

"Let the message about Christ, in all its richness, fill your lives.
Teach and counsel each other with all the wisdom he gives.
Sing psalms and hymns and spiritual songs
to God with thankful hearts.
And whatever you do or say,
do it as a representative of the Lord Jesus,
giving thanks through him to God the Father."
Colossians 3:16-17

• • •

For Me:

- Walk through a mall before it's open. Engage your body and your mind.
- Write a letter to a TV network about a show you don't like — and one you do.
- Reach out to someone who's disappointed you in the past. Let it go and reconnect.

For Others:

- Volunteer at a women's shelter.
- Give a stay-at-home mom the day off.
- Recognize a need of a casual acquaintance and offer to help.

CHAPTER 9

• Difficult People •
(Speak Softly and Carry Chocolate)

*"As iron sharpens iron,
so a friend sharpens a friend."*
Proverbs 27:17

• • •

If everyone thought like I do, the world would be a better place.

Admit it. You've thought this. We all have. We've even considered making it into a sampler to hang in the hall. You think you're the center of the universe. Surprise. So do we. So do two of the new tenants of Peerbaugh Place:

Excerpt from *'Round the Corner*
Chapter 4

"You don't cook?"

"Since you make it sound like a character flaw, I assume you love to cook, right?"

Heddy hadn't meant it that way. *Had she?* "I do like to cook. And bake. It calms me."

The woman turned a chair around and straddled it. "So you need calming?"

"No! I mean, I'm fine. Everything's fine."

"Methinks the lady protests too much . . . Back to your need to be calmed down."

"That's not what I said. I never said that."

"You said cooking calms you."

"A generic comment. It doesn't imply that I'm agitated."

Gail's smile was smug. "You're agitated now."

"Only because you're goading me."

Gail put a hand to her chest. "Me? Goading? How dare I do such a thing?"

Why did everything Gail say come out as a challenge, like a fencer taking a stance? She would not be drawn to this woman's level. Why, Gail didn't even know how to wear makeup. And her ridiculous boy-length hair . . .

Gail gripped the back of the chair and rested her chin on her hands, peering at Heddy too intently. "You're making a judgment against me. I can tell."

Flustered and now disconcerted, Heddy wondered what would be next. "I am doing no such thing."

Gail sat up. "Sure you are. I saw your eyes taking me in, and your mouth—" Gail made a curlicue with her finger. "It went down at the corners, as if what you saw was distasteful. Sorry I don't meet your standards."

Heddy moved to the sink and got herself a glass of water. She didn't like being face to face with Gail, but also didn't like the feeling of having her back exposed.

"You're ignoring me," Gail said.

Heddy realized she was still holding the half-eaten apple. It was the apple's fault. If only she'd gone upstairs as soon as she'd said her greetings to the group in the dining room. She tossed the fruit in the trash.

She heard Gail stand. "Well then. I see how it's going to be around here . . ."

We don't have to ask you to list the difficult people in your life. You know who they are, and they know who they are. The question is: What are you going to do about it?

The surprise answer might be: nothing.

Here's an example: Your child comes home complaining about a teacher who's too hard, too strict, too everything. Your first instinct is to tell your honey-bunny child everything will be all right, Mommy will take care of it.

Don't do it.

The proper response is (and repeat this, looking in a mirror, if necessary): "I'm sorry honey-bunny, but there's nothing I can do. Sometimes you just have to live with difficult people."

Upon saying these words, please remember to apply them

to the difficult people in your own life.

Remember Proverbs 16:22: "Discretion is a life-giving fountain to those who possess it, but discipline is wasted on fools."

Q: What pushes your buttons? (If you have a lengthy list, you'd better do some mighty soul-searching, sister-girl.)

_____
_____
_____
_____
_____
_____
_____

Q: Are any of these pet peeves justified?

_____
_____
_____
_____
_____
_____
_____

Q: What do you do to push other people's buttons? (It's equal-time time.)

_____
_____
_____
_____
_____
_____
_____
_____

Regarding difficult people . . . isn't it time to step back and ask yourself if you are the problem? Maybe. Maybe not. Be honest.

There is also a difference in dealing with difficult friends and coworkers versus dealing with difficult relatives. You may be able to laugh through the frustration of sitting next to a choir member who's always a half-step flat, but find it harder to deal with the in-law who truly meddles.

If you can't ignore the problem person, your choices are fight or flight. Each choice has physical, emotional, and spiritual ramifications: you can make your-self sick, you can make things worse, and you can pull away from God. Think it through. Use your noggin first, not after the fact. Approach the fight or flight decision with love. First Corinthians 13:3 says, "If I gave everything I have to the poor and even sacrificed my body, I could boast about it; but if I didn't love others, I would have gained nothing." Love changes everything — if given a chance.

It's also good to learn how to read your own emotional barometer. If you're stressed, don't choose that particular time to make your weekly phone call to your mom. You know you won't be able to handle it when she tells you (for the 456th time) how to get your laundry *really* clean.

Our goal is to peacefully coexist, look to the ways we're the same, not different. Be smart about it, sister. You can do it.

• • •

God's Word Says:

"O people, the Lord has told you what is good,
and this is what he requires of you:
to do what is right, to love mercy,
and to walk humbly with your God."
Micah 6:8

Q: Have you chosen to ignore — in order to avoid confrontation — a situation with a difficult person? Did it help or make things worse?

_____

_____

_____

_____

_____

_____

_____

_____

_____

_____

If you are a Server Sister — always on the frontline, helping — you will have plenty of opportunities to deal with difficult people. Sisters *will* disappoint you. We cannot completely eliminate or avoid difficult people. Like disappointment, it's a fact of life. But we don't have to become a difficult person to survive. In fact, there's the possibility that we can actually learn something from these people. We're not always right, you know. God has put them in our lives for a reason.

Find it.

• • •

Hunger and Thirst:

"God has given each of you a gift
from his great variety of spiritual gifts.
Use them well to serve one another."
1 Peter 4:10

"The Lord approves of those who are good,
but he condemns those who plan wickedness.
Wickedness never brings stability, but the godly have deep roots."
Proverbs 12:2-3

*"For once you were full of darkness,
but now you have light from the Lord.
So live as people of light! For this light within you produces
only what is good and right and true."*
Ephesians 5:8-9

*"Come quickly, Lord, and answer me, for my depression deepens.
Don't turn away from me, or I will die.
Let me hear of your unfailing love each morning,
for I am trusting you.
Show me where to walk, for I give myself to you.
Rescue me from my enemies, Lord; I run to you to hide me.
Teach me to do your will, for you are my God.
May your gracious Spirit lead me forward on a firm footing.
For the glory of your name, O Lord, preserve my life.
Because of your faithfulness, bring me out of this distress.
In your unfailing love, silence all my enemies
and destroy all my foes, for I am your servant."*
Psalm 143:7-12

*"So don't worry about these things, saying,
'What will we eat? What will we drink? What will we wear?'
These things dominate the thoughts of unbelievers,
but your heavenly Father already knows all your needs.
Seek the Kingdom of God above all else, and live righteously,
and he will give you everything you need.
So don't worry about tomorrow,
for tomorrow will bring its own worries.
Today's trouble is enough for today."*
Matthew 6:31-33

• • •

For Me:

- Buy new sheets or towels.
- Have a mend-fences picnic and invite a difficult person in your life to attend.
- Organize a closet. Organization is a great outlet for frustration.

For Others:

- Volunteer at a hospital.
- Help with an organization's fund-raising activities.
- Get involved with a political campaign.

CHAPTER 10

• Resolving Conflict •
(Swinging From an Olive Branch)

"How wonderful and pleasant it is
when [sisters] live together in harmony!"
Psalm 133:1

• • •

Moving on from our discussion of difficult people . . . *You say po-tato, I say po-tah-to* . . . Brenda likes mashed, Nancy prefers French-fries. Does it really matter? The conflicts in your life may not be this simple, but when you look at the root cause of disagreements, it's often something that doesn't really matter.

The way we deal with conflict is influenced by our personality. But remember sisters, it takes two to tango (and tangle). There *is* the personality of the other person to consider. Or more than one.

For example, we all know the potential for conflict when you put a lot of women together. As conflict looms at Peerbaugh Place, Mae proclaims, "Take your corners, sisters!"

Excerpt from *The Sister Circle*
Chapter 6

"You can't have people over, *I'm* having people over," Tessa said.

"When did this happen?" Mae asked.

"This afternoon while I was at class. We were discussing Elizabethan history and how Walsingham—"

"Walsing-who?"

Tessa's back straightened. "Sir Francis Walsingham. He was the secretary of state to Queen Elizabeth the first and developed a secret service of sorts that purged the queen of her enemies. Quite ruthless, but very loyal."

"Sounds like a fun guy."

Tessa pursed her lips. "He's an interesting man. Which is why I have three friends coming over at seven to continue our discussion." She nodded toward the batter. "I'm making fruit meringues."

Summer spoke over her shoulder. "We don't get any."

Tessa flashed the little girl a look that surprised Evelyn. But Summer took it well by turning back to her work.

"Well," Mae said. "Everyone can have as much of my food offering as they want." She moved to the sink to wash the celery.

Tessa had not moved and the spatula threatened to drip into her hand. "But you don't understand. This is not acceptable. We can't both have people over at the same time."

"Afraid we'll corrupt your discussion, Tessie? Bring in some of the rebellious Irish influence from my Fitzpatrick name?"

Evelyn tensed as Tessa did a quarter turn in her direction. "What are *you* going to do about this situation?"

Mae did her own quarter turn, but added a smile. "Yes, Evelyn, what *are* you going to do about this *situation?*"

"I . . . I don't really know what—"

Audra came through the door, her eyes seeking her daughter. "Hey, baby. Did you have a good day?"

"It was great, Mommy. We cooked and cleaned."

Evelyn was glad to change the subject. "How was work?"

"Oh, it was—"

"Excuse me?" Tessa said. "We have a crisis here."

Audra scanned their faces. "What's going on?"

Mae did the honors. "It seems Tessie and I are engaged in a battle for the parlor. She's invited three of her snooty scholar types over to discuss dead people, and I've invited three of my fabulously amiable friends over to play cards, and—"

Audra put a hand to her mouth. "And I've invited Gillie and Piper over to watch a movie."

"This—" Tessa punctuated the air with the spatula

once, spraying a blob of meringue onto the floor. Her hand returned to its place beneath it. "This will not do."

Evelyn wanted to flee. "Oh dear."

Mae stepped into the middle of the kitchen, her hands raised. "Take your corners, sisters. We *will* work this out."

"I don't see how."

Mae pointed a finger at Tessa. "Would you and your group be comfortable in the sunroom?"

Tessa glanced toward the room at the back of the house off the kitchen. It was clearly not her first choice. "I was hoping for the parlor. After all, that *is* the most elegant—"

"I won't argue with you there. But my friends and I need a table. If we use the dining room and Audra and her bunch watch a movie in the parlor where the TV is located . . ." Mae dropped her chin and challenged Tessa. "Unless you and your friends wouldn't mind the sounds of a hearty card game rising from the next room?"

Tessa opened her mouth, then shut it, then opened it again. "You're not giving me much choice."

Mae shrugged. "Yeah, well . . ."

Tessa shuffled her shoulders. "I want a choice."

Mae dropped her jaw. " You have a choice. You can either join our card game in the dining room or watch a movie in the parlor. Or you can have your meeting in the relative quiet of the sunroom. Take your pick."

Tessa's eyes flashed. "What happened to the democracy of Peerbaugh Place? Since when does one tenant get to dictate—"

"But you want to dictate—"

Tessa looked surprised. "Me?"

Mae took a step toward her, brandishing a celery stalk. "Who has proclaimed herself the dictator of this house from the first moment she—?"

"I did no such—"

Audra moved between them. "Ladies!"

Mae lowered the celery. "She always has to have her way."

"Only because my way is the best way."

Mae's snicker was thick with contempt. "Our own little Napoleon. How did we get so lucky?"

"Technically, Napoleon was not a dictator. He was an emperor and—"

Mae raised her arms in a mock bow. "Oh, Empress

Tessie, how may we serve you?"

Audra pulled one of Mae's hands down. "Come on now, you two. We can work this out."

"Not me," Mae said. She suddenly took a musketeer stance with the celery as her sword. "I say *en garde!*"

When Tessa picked up a spoon, Evelyn fled the room. This was ridiculous. She headed to the solace of the front porch. When no one followed to offer their apologies, her anger grew. They were completely missing the point. It didn't matter who used what room— the point was that not one of them had even asked permission to use *any* room. After all, it was her house.

She looked toward the kitchen where loud voices could still be heard. At least, it used to be her house.

Q: Which resident of Peerbaugh Place are you rooting for? Rooting against?

_____

_____

_____

_____

_____

Brenda supports Mae. Nancy (who hates conflict) sides with Evelyn and is heading to her own porch right now.

We've been told that learning to resolve conflict requires an understanding of why we do what we do. We beg to differ. If we knew why we do what we do, we wouldn't do what we do. (Say that fast three times.)

Here are four methods of dealing with conflict:

The Avoider: Because they'd rather go to the dentist than deal with conflict, avoiders like to pretend nothing ever happened. And when they realize it isn't going away, they want to escape. Isn't it amazing how creative they can be when it comes to avoiding someone? They sit on the opposite side of church, or convince themselves they can skip Book Club this week. But what does this get the Avoider? Nada. Nothing is ever resolved. Their little world of perfect is an illusion.

The Attacker: "Attack" doesn't have to mean being physically aggressive. Passive-aggressive behavior is also a tactic of The Attacker. Withdrawing their affection or their touch can be just as affective. And words? Words cut and make people bleed inside. Attackers are well aware of the satisfaction that comes from being the tour guide on a guilt trip. And what about hearing these often condescending last words: I'll pray for you. Yikes. The bad part about handling conflict through attacks is that no one wins, nothing is resolved, feelings are hurt, and the chasm between attacker and victim remains.

The Adjuster: If only we could. Being able to compromise and make necessary changes during the conflict is an art that can be learned (send $99 to getagrip.com for your handy-dandy correspondence course). The hard part stems from the fact that this method requires maturity and stability from all involved. Don't look at us. We've tried to think of personal illustrations for this method and have come up empty. Make your own conclusions about this category we can't claim. Let's all try harder, sisters.

The Accepter: Sometimes it's easier to handle conflict by just accepting it. The conflict happened. It's not worth blowing your diet over. This is definitely one of those "good news, bad news" scenarios. The good news is when it really doesn't matter, great! It's over. The bad news is when it does matter, it's just a matter of time before the whole thing resurfaces.

Q: Which method of dealing with conflict do you use most often?

_____

_____

_____

_____

_____

_____

The cause of the conflict is of varied importance. But the method of resolving it has lasting impact on our relationships with others. Through trial and error, we create a pattern of behavior that works for us. Right or wrong. Unfortunately, many of us have edged and hedged and wedged our whole lives while dealing with conflict — or trying to avoid it. At this point, the Fixer Sister might be able to help. She's good at sorting things out. Though she's often gruff, be patient with her — she might have good advice. Logic *can* be a good thing.

Q: **Think of a time you dealt with conflict well and a time you didn't. Why did things turn out the way they did? How could you have changed your response to make it turn out better?**

_____
_____
_____
_____
_____
_____
_____
_____

Because you are such savvy sisters, you probably realize by now that we have not said anything profound about "resolving conflict." The truth is, each person must find her own unique method. Plus, sometimes the conflict is self-inflicted — which is an entirely different kettle of potatoes.

Strengths and weaknesses aside, remember we're not in this alone. There is a time for conflict and a time for peace, and our God is the Father of them both. Seek Him for guidance. He knows *just* how to handle it and will even give you *just* the right words at *just* the right time. Pray first, speak second. In fact, in times of intense conflict, we've found that specifically praying, "Lord, help me not say anything you don't approve of" is a lifesaver. Funny how He often nudges us into saying nothing. Wave the white flag of surrender — to Him.

• • •

Hunger and Thirst

"So humble yourselves under the mighty power of God,
and at the right time he will lift you up in honor.
Give all your worries and cares to God,
for he cares about you. Stay alert!
Watch out for your great enemy, the devil.
He prowls around like a roaring lion, looking for someone to devour.
Stand firm against him, and be strong in your faith.
Remember that your Christian brothers and sisters
all over the world are going through
the same kind of suffering you are.
In his kindness God called you to share in his eternal glory
by means of Christ Jesus. So after you have suffered a little while,
he will restore, support, and strengthen you, and he will place you on
a firm foundation. All power to him forever! Amen."
1 Peter 5:6-11

"For I can do everything
through Christ who gives me strength."
Philippians 4:13

"Make sure that the light you think you have
is not actually darkness.
If you are filled with light, with no dark corners,
then your whole life will be radiant,
as though a floodlight were filling you with light."
Luke 11:35-36

"But someone who does not know, and then does something wrong,
will be punished only lightly. When someone has been given much,
much will be required in return; and when someone has been
entrusted with much, even more will be required."
Luke 12:48

• • •

For Me:

- Get your kitchen clean by trading duties with a friend—clean each other's kitchens!
- Play a card game for jelly beans (no arguing! I get the red ones!)
- Go antique shopping for something older than you are—and don't gloat.

For Others:

- Think of a creative way to initiate a scholarship-fund for a day-care center so single mothers can re-enter the work force.
- Make an anonymous donation to a crisis phone line, or volunteer to help others handle conflict.
- Offer to help with church maintenance to prevent complaints and conflict.

CHAPTER 11

• Disappointment •
(As Inevitable as Calories and Taxes)

*"You have to change the way you think
to change the way you feel."*
Nancy and Brenda

• • •

After long deliberation, much study and prayer, we have decided that the key to handling disappointment comes down to this one bit of wisdom:

Deal with it.

We really wanted to leave you with just that thought — deal with it — but some of our friends felt we were not taking the emotion of disappointment seriously enough. So here's our next thought, borne of experience: times of suffering through disappointment are often times when we grow the most. If we never had such times, we'd be robots. Mindless, feeling-less Stepford women with stiff hair and Barbie-sized waistlines.

We need to keep in mind that disappointment is frequently the result of taking everything too seriously — including ourselves. Finding a proper level of confidence in who we are and who God created us to be comes from within, through the Holy Spirit's guidance. Ask God to show you your true identity. "For the Lord sees every heart and knows every plan and thought. If you seek him, you will find him" (1 Chronicles 28:9).

Most disappointments involve another person. We can suffer disappointment due to our children, our marriage or singleness, our careers . . . Disappointment often comes from trying to plan someone else's life or wanting them to live up to our standards and expectations. Nancy imagined having children who were involved in the theater, who loved to sing like she did. She has three children and none have interest in these areas. That was hard to take at first, until she realized they have other abilities that make them unique. Bottom line: "They are not me."

Brenda reminded her that the world doesn't need another Von Trapp family anyway—and Edelweiss doesn't grow in Kansas.

Remember when your mother hated that hippie outfit you wore to college? Or disapproved of the classes you were taking, or the kind of music you liked? These are many of the issues that disappoint us about our own kids now. Love past that. Pick your battles.

Every sister will deal with disappointment differently, and no matter how you identify yourself, Soul Sister, Rah-Rah Sister, Giver Sister… a friend who demonstrates a different way of expressing themselves, a different way of seeing life, is sure to disappoint you. The hardest lesson about getting along is realizing that each person is unique and their main purpose in life is not to satisfy our criteria and jump through our hoops. We must let God's criteria for a meaningful existence rise above ours. We must learn to love unconditionally as Christ loves us.

Witness Mae's disappointment in how her son chose to get married, and feel with her as she is challenged to love unconditionally.

Excerpt from *An Undivided Heart,*
Chapter 16

The phone rang. Mae answered. "Ringo! Just the man I need to talk to. I've been working on the wedding and you have some decisions to make and—"

"I have something to tell you, Mom."

Mae's heart did a nosedive. "Are you okay? Is Soon-ja—?"

"We're pregnant."

Mae found a chair and sat in it. Old adages sprang to mind: *Putting the cart before the horse. A bun in the oven. Shotgun wedding . . .*

Being a grandmother.

But before she could voice any of these feelings, Ringo said, "We're also married."

She was glad she was sitting down. The table was still covered with wedding books. Maybe she'd heard wrong. "You're *going* to get—"

"No, Mom. We got married. We eloped."

She pulled in a breath. "You can't do that. I'm planning a wedding here. I picked out dresses and invitations and flowers and—"

"You'll have to use your ideas for Starr's wedding. Whenever. If ever . . ."

Fat chance. "Why didn't you wait? We could have moved the date up. You could have had a beautiful ceremony."

"Once Soon-ja found out, she was devastated. Her family back in Korea is very strict. She felt shame."

Having come from a hippie, free-love lifestyle, Mae had trouble taking a strong stand on premarital anything.

"Soon-ja insisted on being married immediately. For their sake. I couldn't argue with her. I want her to be happy."

Mae was moved by the devotion in her son's voice. She wished she could be assured that her own voice wouldn't be whiny with disappointment. This was an important moment in her son's life. She needed to respond correctly. *Lord, help me . . .*

"Mom?"

She cleared her throat. "I'm here. I was just thinking."

"What?" His guard was up.

"You're not going to make the child call me Nana Mae, are you? Because that sounds like a goat's name."

He laughed. "What would you like to be called?"

Grandmother was too sophisticated for her taste, *Grammy* too country. "How about Grandma?"

"You got it."

Those of us who are mothers can imagine how Mae felt. Yet she stopped herself from saying what was truly on her mind. She did the right thing. She kept the line of communication open between herself and her son. She . . .

dealt with it.

Dealing with her disappointment was not a once and for all, over-with forever, process for Mae. Her disappointment hurt and would hurt for a long while. But Mae faced the reality that for now her disappointment had to give way to celebrating the new little life that would grace their family. We know it's hard to let go of disappointment, but you can do it. Be kind. Be magnanimous. Be the gracious woman God made you to be.

Another kind of disappointment can result from misplaced confidence. Now be honest, you bought that widget offered on TV because you truly believed the claims that it would simplify everything you did in your kitchen and allow you to create appetizing and attractive meals in less than ten minutes. And when you bought one, they threw in a second one for free. What a deal.

Come on sister, did you really believe that? You wanted to believe what you were hearing. And fess up. How many face creams and make-up items have you purchased because you wanted to believe their claims that you could look years younger and movie-star beautiful.

We can throw away widgets and face creams that don't work and the cost won't put us into bankruptcy, but when it comes to disappointment in people, it's different. Disappointment can bankrupt us emotionally, physically, and spiritually.

Remember our simplistic answer of "Just deal with it"? Here's an idea for you. Right now, mentally figure out how you are going to "deal with it." Make a plan. Then every time you have a deposit of disappointment in your brain-bank, implement that plan.

Brenda has a checklist she uses (she really is a Lister Sister). She also gives herself a time frame to brood and fret over her disappointment. Then she gives it to God and gets on with life.

Nancy needs to be alone to deal with disappointment. She goes for a drive or a walk, needing to pinpoint exactly *why* she's disappointed (definitely a Soul Sister). Then she too gives it up to God and asks Him to handle it. Only after going through this process is she able to move on. Not that it doesn't still hurt. As with Mae, dealing with disappointment isn't instantaneous. But getting past the first painful acknowledgment of the problem is an important initial step toward acceptance. And healing.

• • •

God's Word Says:

"We can rejoice, too, when we run into problems and trials,
for we know that they help us develop endurance.
And endurance develops strength of character,
and character strengthens our confident hope of salvation.
And this hope will not lead to disappointment.
For we know how dearly God loves us, because he has given us the
Holy Spirit to fill our hearts with his love."
Romans 5:3-5

Q: How do you handle disappointment? (Does your method work?)

_____

_____

_____

_____

_____

_____

Q: How might you better handle disappointment — a way better suited to your personality?

_____

_____

_____

_____

_____

_____

_____

Ultimately, disappointments are burdens we don't need to carry. Give them to God and get on with life. "Jesus said, 'Come to me, all of you who are weary and carry heavy burdens, and I will give you rest. Take my yoke upon you. Let me teach you, because I am humble and gentle at heart, and you will find rest for your souls. For my yoke is easy to bear, and the burden I give you is light.'" (Matthew 11:28-30).

• • •

Hunger and Thirst:

"Dear brothers and sisters, when troubles come your way,
consider it an opportunity for great joy.
For you know that when your faith is tested,
your endurance has a chance to grow.
So let it grow, for when your endurance is fully developed,
you will be perfect and complete, needing nothing.
If you need wisdom, ask our generous God, and he will give it to you.
He will not rebuke you for asking. But when you ask him,
be sure that your faith is in God alone. Do not waver,
for a person with divided loyalty is as unsettled as a wave of the sea
that is blown and tossed by the wind.
James 1: 2-6

"Trust in the Lord with all your heart;
do not depend on your own understanding.
Seek his will in all you do, and he will show you which path to take."
Proverbs 3:5-6

"Submit to God, and you will have peace;
then things will go well for you.
Listen to his instructions, and store them in your heart.
If you return to the Almighty, you will be restored —
so clean up your life. If you give up your lust for money
and throw your precious gold into the river,
the Almighty himself will be your treasure.
He will be your precious silver!
Then you will take delight in the Almighty and look up to God.

You will pray to him,
and he will hear you, and you will fulfill your vows to him.
You will succeed in whatever you choose to do,
and light will shine on the road ahead of you.
If people are in trouble and you say, `Help them,' God will save them.
Even sinners will be rescued;
they will be rescued because your hands are pure."
Job 22:21-30

• • •

For Me:

- Put on your "big girl" panties, and deal with it —
  whatever *it* is. (Buying yourself a pretty pair helps.)
- Make a list of all your blessings and trials, then thank
  God for every one.
- Go to a spa, a movie, or to a play — or just play!

For Others:

- Write a note to your children telling them you are
  proud to be their mother. Or a note to your husband,
  your parents, or a friend.
- Listen. That's it. Be a sister to a sister. Listen.
  Encourage. Comfort. Love.
- Think of something a friend or loved one has been
  wanting for a long time and make it happen.

CHAPTER 12

• Forgiveness •
(I Will If You Will)

"If you forgive those who sin against you,
your heavenly Father will forgive you.
But if you refuse to forgive others,
your Father will not forgive your sins."
Matthew 6:14-15

• • •

Forgiveness is not a two-way street. Rarely do you sit across the table from some-body and agree to forgive or be forgiven.

Luckily, you can do it incognito. Yet there are times it is appropriate to go face-to-face and make things right.

In the excerpt below, Evelyn suddenly finds herself talking about her late husband and their less-than-perfect marriage in a bitter tirade to her friend, Wayne.

Excerpt from *An Undivided Heart*
Chapter 18

"Talk to me, Evelyn. Let me help you get through this."
She blew her nose. "It won't help. He's gone."
But maybe it *will* help. Aaron's been gone quite a while, so for you to still harbor this bitterness about your life . . . it can't be healthy."
Her laugh oozed bitterness, a sickening sound. "What good will it do to talk about all we *didn't* have, all we *didn't* feel? Especially to someone like you, who lost your soul mate after sharing a great marriage. You, who have no regrets, who isn't disgusted by the memory of who you

were when you were together." The tears started fresh. She was glad he didn't say anything. She looked out the passenger window and let herself cry. "Why can't I remember anything good about him? Why can't I remember anything good about myself *with* him?"

"I'm sure it's not that bad."

She whipped toward him. "I wanted him to be out of my life! And he died! Don't you understand that? I'm responsible!" Her voice rang in the car. The look on Wayne's face made her fumble for the door handle. She got the door open and tumbled out, tripping on the gravel. She fell to the ground and felt the sting of rocks against her palms.

Suddenly he was at her side, on the ground himself, cradling her in his arms.

A car whizzed past and honked.

I'm making a fool of myself collided with *I don't care. Just hold me, Wayne. Make it all go away. Make the hurt go away.*

He whispered a soft, "Shh, shh" in her ear. She dug her face into his chest, not wanting the world to see her shame; not wanting to see the world. He rocked her until her tears were spent.

He helped her to her feet and led her to a picnic table beneath a crimson pin oak, its leaves holding on far beyond when other trees had given up their bounty. She sat on the bench, facing out. He sat beside her, his arm keeping her close. Safe. Crickets chirped. The air was cool against her hot cheeks. Her insides felt hollow, as if there was nothing left, as if it had all been scraped clean. She looked down at her bloodied hands as if they belonged to someone else. But no. They were hers. *Her* scars for *her* sin.

Wayne reached over and lifted her chin, but instead of turning it toward himself, he turned her focus toward the west. "Look, Evelyn. Look at the sky getting ready for the sunset."

The sky was an artist's palate with sweeping swaths of reds, purples, and blues. Azure puffs against white with the globe of the sun getting ready to be cut in two by the horizon. It was moving on past today, getting ready for its journey to tomorrow when it would come up fresh and new. Cleansed. Warm. Its light so pure and intense that one dare not look at it.

"The day is nearly done," Wayne said. "Let it go."

She watched the sky. "But—"

"No. Forgive him. Forgive yourself."

"But I hated—"

"Hated. Past tense. Hate no more. Not Aaron, not your old life, not the old you. God forgives you. He forgives Aaron. He's made things fresh and clean."

Evelyn's throat tightened. "But I don't deserve to be fresh and clean. I—"

"No, you don't. Neither do I. Neither do any of us. But Jesus forgives you—whether you want Him to or not. His work was done on the cross. He's not taking it back. It's a done deal. Just accept it. Accept His love and forgiveness as a gift; as a way to look forward, to move on."

She filled her emptiness with a deep breath of cool November air. "How can I refuse?"

He laughed. "You can't."

She put her head against his shoulder and they watched the sun disappear from today. Forever.

The need—the opportunity—to forgive can come to us daily. From the small stuff like your husband not getting gas in the car when he'd promised, to the larger issue of a friend sharing a confidence she'd promised to keep secret. We are called by God to forgive. Not just once, but as many times as it takes. It's not a suggestion. It's a direct instruction from Jesus to all of us:

• • •

God's Word Says:

Then Peter came to him and asked, "Lord, how often should I forgive someone who sins against me? Seven times?"
"No, not seven times," Jesus replied, "but seventy times seven!"
Matthew 18:21-22

The blessing of forgiveness is that it benefits us, the forgiver, just as much (if not more) than the one who's being forgiven. It softens our hearts. It draws us closer to God. It makes us better. (So if we've said anything to offend you in this book, forgive us.)

Note that Jesus doesn't ask us to forget. Just forgive. So let the past go, and forget enough to look forward instead of back.

Q: Who do you need to forgive? For what?

_____
_____
_____
_____
_____
_____
_____
_____
_____
_____

Q: What steps can you take to move toward forgiveness?

_____
_____
_____
_____
_____
_____
_____
_____

Whether we feel shame for something we've done or we feel guilty for not forgiving someone, if we don't deal with the forgiveness, it can become an oozing wound that a Band-Aid won't fix.

It's not easy. We often keep tabs on faults and mistakes (the current score is Brenda 12, Nancy 0). We're very hard on each other — and ourselves. The Rah-Rah Sister has a great advantage in the area of forgiveness. She can easily say I'm sorry and move on to enjoy life. Take a lesson.

Actually, healing can only truly start when we forgive ourselves. If you can't forgive yourself for the mistakes you've made, how can you genuinely forgive other people? How can you extend what you don't have? And don't think what you've done is unforgivable. Is what you've done so bad that Jesus' death on the cross is not enough? How dare you think that! Healing can only begin after we confess our sins to God, accept His forgiveness, and forgive ourselves.

An unforgiving spirit breeds bitterness, and a bitter woman is not capable of living the life God designed for her. Plus, she's a pain to be around—just ask her family. Is all this angst God's fault? Too many times God *is* blamed.

So . . . what's done is done. The joy and release that comes when you can forgive yourself and others is divine—truly "Capital D"—Divine.

Forgiving is a necessity. It's our duty *and* our privilege. Does the person we need to forgive deserve it? Do we? Probably not, but that doesn't matter. After all, Christ died on the cross to forgive all of our sins: past, present, and future. Isn't that amazing? And humbling?

'Nuf said.

• • •

Hunger and Thirst

"Make allowance for each other's faults,
and forgive anyone who offends you.
Remember, the Lord forgave you, so you must forgive others.
Above all, clothe yourselves with love,
which binds us all together in perfect harmony.
And let the peace that comes from Christ rule in your hearts.
For as members of one body you are called to live in peace.
And always be thankful."
Colossians 3:13-15

"If your enemies are hungry, give them food to eat.
If they are thirsty, give them water to drink.
You will heap burning coals of shame on their heads,
and the Lord will reward you."
Proverbs 25:21-22

"Sensible people control their temper;
they earn respect by overlooking wrongs."
Proverbs 19:11

"You have heard the law that says,
'Love your neighbor' and hate your enemy.
But I say, love your enemies! Pray for those who persecute you!
In that way, you will be acting as true children
of your Father in heaven.
For he gives his sunlight to both the evil and the good,
and he sends rain on the just and the unjust alike.
If you love only those who love you, what reward is there for that?
Even corrupt tax collectors do that much.
If you are kind only to your friends,
how are you different from anyone else?
Even pagans do that. But you are to be perfect,
even as your Father in heaven is perfect."
Matthew 5:43-48

"God blesses those who are merciful,
for they will be shown mercy."
Matthew 5:7

• • •

For Me:

- Make your favorite dessert and savor every bite.
- Go on a private mini-retreat and make things right with God (a local bed and breakfast is good).
- Make a list of the good things you've done through relationships and think of ways to do more.

For Others:

- On the special days of your life (when you usually receive a gift) give a gift to someone in need anonymously.
- Contact a person who needs your forgiveness.
- Contact a person who needs to forgive you.

CHAPTER 13

• Courage •
(You Go, Girl!)

*"For God has not given us a spirit of fear and timidity,
but of power, love, and self-discipline."*
2 Timothy 1:7

• • •

The woman thinks she knows everything . . .

You know the kind. She knows the best places to shop, has the best hairdresser, is on the best diet, and has connections to hook you up with the absolutely best places to go for any la-di-da social event. She makes you want to put twenty tacky pink plastic flamingos in her yard and then call the paper to feature it on the front page.

The headline will read: *Local Woman Stunned by Foreign Objects: admits SHE DOESN'T KNOW where they came from.*

Are we naughty, or what?

The phrase, "All I know is I know nothing," is one of the most courageous statements ever made. The need to be honest with ourselves is tough but necessary to develop the courage to become all we can be.

Witness a discouraged Evelyn, in bed alone, calling out to her deceased husband:

Excerpt from *'Round the Corner*
Chapter 8

"Oh, Aaron . . ."
She hadn't meant to call out for her late husband. And in truth, Evelyn was getting her grief under control quite nicely.

But every once in a while, her need for him pounced, demanding attention, nudging her, prodding her, just like *he* used to do, pestering her until she paid him his due.

And though she hadn't been particularly happy in the last few years of their marriage, she did miss Aaron's companionship. The sound of his familiar voice, the Old Spice smell of him, and the comfort of his constant presence, always there, no matter what. At the time, she'd considered that more of an annoyance than a blessing — until he wasn't there at all. Now, annoying would be a welcome change from the isolation she suffered.

She rolled to her back and stared at the ceiling, her eyes skimming the faint swirls of the texturing. Even though her life was inhabited by others, she was isolated. She was the only widow. She was the only grandmother. She was the only one who had no clue as to why she was alive, why she was here.

This last idea overwhelmed her.

Pray for your direction, Evelyn.

She sat up in bed, pulling the pillow to her lap. Why had she not thought of this? Why had she never thought about asking God point-blank to show her His plan for her life? Everybody else was off on their own roads, tooling along as if everything was so clear, yet Evelyn was stuck on the shoulder, sitting there waiting. For what?

She remembered Aaron's tendency to never ask directions. Up until now she'd been exactly like him. But no more. No more!

She tossed the pillow aside and got out of bed, falling to her knees beside it. She clasped her hands and drew them to her forehead. "Lord? Piper and Audra and even Mae have said that everyone has a unique purpose. I hope that's true. And if it's true, then I want to know what my purpose is. Why did You make me? Why am I here, now, in this place and time? What do You want me to do with the rest of my life? Show me. Please?"

She waited a few moments in silence, hoping — but not expecting — God to make some brilliant idea pop into her mind. Nothing happened.

And yet...as Evelyn stood to get dressed, she did feel different. Hopeful. Exhilarated. As if something fantastic was promised, even if the details weren't known. And she found that flame of anticipation very, very warm, a fire that could fuel her through the hours and days that were her life.

Admitting uncertainty about your life is not an act of weakness but can be the first spark of courage. Think of women who have accomplished great things. Diplomats negotiating peace, great-grandmothers getting college diplomas, artists creating beauty, volunteers changing lives . . . At some point each one felt a spark of courage and fanned the flame. But sparks can go out. Courage is a choice.

Q: When you were young, what did you always want to be when you grew up?

_____
_____
_____
_____
_____

Q: What are your dreams now?

_____
_____
_____
_____
_____
_____
_____
_____

Q: What's holding you back?

_____
_____
_____
_____
_____
_____
_____
_____

We're asking you to be courageous, right now. Set aside the woman you've been and think of yourself in a new, exciting way—God's way. Often when we start gaining confidence in our purpose, by taking the simple step of admitting we *have* a unique purpose, our attitude changes. We change.

But it's risky.

Perhaps we've been sampling our real purpose for years, and have even become accustomed to its slightly bland taste, thinking what we were doing was as good as it gets. Know this: There's more. When we let God season our purpose with his salt, it—and we—come alive, and there's no going back. Ever. Once our taste buds have been whetted with this new seasoning of life, we crave more and get more adventurous toward trying something new. With God empowering us, our lives become a feast of purpose, a banquet of opportunities.

Read these verses carefully; read them aloud. And to claim them for *your* life, insert your name in the blanks:

• • •

God's Word Says:

_____ *is the salt of the earth.*
But what good is salt if it has lost its flavor?
Can you make it salty again?
It will be thrown out and trampled underfoot as worthless.
_____ *is the light of the world —*
like a city on a hilltop, that cannot be hidden.
No one lights a lamp and then puts it under a basket.
Instead, a lamp is placed on a stand,
where it gives light to everyone in the house.
In the same way, let _____*'s good deeds*
shine out for all to see, so that everyone will praise
_____ *'s heavenly Father.*
Matthew 5:13-16

Do you feel the power in those verses? They become a prayer. In fact, say them again. Pray them again.

God is telling *you* to spice up the world, don't blend in, but season it in order to bring out its best.

One more thing: You may have some God-given abilities hidden under a basket. Let them out. Let them shine for His glory. We dare not lose our flavor or dull our light. Too much is at stake.

Q: What are your God-given abilities? (Now is not the time to be shy.)

_____
_____
_____
_____
_____
_____
_____

Q: What's the basket that hides your abilities made of? (Fear, false humility, timidity, hesitancy, arrogance, procrastination, panic, selfishness, feeling incompetent?)

_____
_____
_____
_____
_____

Q: How can you remove your basket?

_____
_____
_____
_____
_____

Q: For fun . . . if you were a seasoning sprinkled on the world, would you be: salt? cayenne pepper? cinnamon?

_____

_____

_____

_____

_____

When it comes to courage . . . every sister needs to be a Giver Sister. What God asks each of us to give is ourselves, surrendered to Him. You may not have money, possessions, time, or energy to give, but give *yourself* and see what God does with you.

We need to be confident that God didn't make a mistake in creating us. And through that self-confidence — confidence based on Him — we can fulfill God's purpose, be bold, and achieve our dreams. So don't waste another moment wandering. Pray for Him to show you your purpose. Pray Psalm 138:8 comes true: "The Lord will work out His plans for my life." Not *might*. WILL. If you let Him.

• • •

God's Word Says:

"Show me the right path, O Lord;
point out the road for me to follow.
Lead me by your truth and teach me,
for you are the God who saves me.
All day long I put my hope in you."
Psalm 25:4-5

And we — Brenda and Nancy — are putting our hope in you, too. And in each other.

There's a story about a woman who stands before God and asks Him a question: "Father, there's so much sadness and evil in the world; there's so much to be done. Why don't you

105

send someone?" To which God replies, "I did. I sent you."

Did you feel chills at that punch-line? Grab onto those words. Cherish them. And be challenged by them, because it's true.

He sent you.

• • •

God's Word Says:

"Then I heard the Lord asking,
'Whom should I send as a messenger to this people?
Who will go for us?'
I said, 'Here I am. Send me.' "
Isaiah 6:8

So go on. Do something with that amazing blessing, as one woman, and as a special woman joined with your dear friends, as sisters in Christ.

Change the world. We'll be watching for you, rooting for you, and praying for you.

• • •

Hunger and Thirst:

"The Lord replied, 'Look around at the nations; look and be amazed!
For I am doing something in your own day,
something you wouldn't believe even if someone told you about it.'"
Habakkuk 1:5

"I knew you before I formed you in your mother's womb.
Before you were born I set you apart."
Jeremiah 1:5

"The Lord says, 'I will guide you along the best pathway for your life.
I will advise you and watch over you.' "
Psalm 32:8

"Take delight in the Lord,
and he will give you your heart's desires."
Psalm 37:4

• • •

For Me:

- Set aside time to purposefully dream about your future. Dream big.
- Thank God for your dream. Ask Him to help you make it happen.
- Do something tangible toward pursuing your dream.

For Others:

- Speak to those closest to you about your dream—and theirs. See each other's vision and dream together. Pray together.
- Offer to help someone else pursue his or her dream.
- Speak out to the world about something you care about.

• It's Party Time! •
(*Ideas for Sister Get-Togethers*)

"For where two or three gather together as my followers,
I am there among them."
Matthew 18:20

It's party time! When you gather a bunch of women together, a party is inevitable. Here are a few party themes for your gatherings. Some of these ideas came from the pages of *The Sister Circle* novels. Some are new. We're not giving you a lot of details because we know you are creative creatures. Have fun. Send pictures.

• • •

Makeover Party
- Bring your makeup and have fun doing each other's makeup.
- Bring baby pictures and guess who's who.
- Go out for lunch when you're in the "after" mode.

• • •

Movie Party
- Dress up as your favorite actress or movie character.
- Pretend it's Oscar night and dress to walk the red carpet (is your speech ready?).
- Get out your good china and crystal and watch a chick-flick.

• • •

Pajama Party

- Go to a bed and breakfast for the night with a bunch of your sisters—or go to someone's house.
- When guests arrive, have them put their pajamas in a paper sack. Later, hold them up one at a time and guess who they belong to (you'd be shocked by what Brenda wears to bed).
- Tell scary stories and share silly secrets.

• • •

Manicure and Pedicure Party

- Serve finger sandwiches or foot-long hot dogs (ha-ha, get the joke?)
- Paint each nail a different color.
- Bring glitter (you take it from there . . .)

• • •

Book Exchange Party

- Wrap a book or two and have a white-elephant exchange.
- Read your favorite passage.
- Brainstorm your own collective book.

• • •

Spice Exchange Party

- Bring your favorite spice and a recipe that uses the spice, plus the food ready to eat (of course!).
- Know something strange or special about the history of the spice.
- Share a creative idea on organizing your spices.

• • •

Cookie Exchange Party

- Bring as many cookies as there are guests (everyone takes one of each—eating along the way).
- Have special sacks for take-home cookies.
- Bring the recipe on an index card (one for each guest).

• • •

Worry Box Party

- Bring an empty recipe box.
- Decorate with stickers, ribbon, photos, sequins . . .
- Get prayed up about each other's concerns, write a note, and place it in the box for God to handle (get updates later regarding God's amazing way of handling your worries).

• • •

Quilting Party

- Bring your scraps or an existing project.
- Bring your favorite quilt pattern and sew them together to create a quilt representing all of you as a whole.
- Exchange stories about the nuts in your family tree.

• • •

International Party

- Come representing your favorite country (try to use the accent).
- Bring music, food, or decorations that fit with your country of choice.
- Share something about a custom or holiday

• • •

Good Old Days Party

- Bring your old yearbooks.
- Bring an old bridesmaid or prom dress (fitting into the dress earns brownie points — or brownies).
- Give prizes for the Worst Dress, Most Horrible Hair, Most Changed, Hottest Babe, Dork Princess, and Prom Queen.

We were going to give you ideas for parties that had an outreach or noble purpose, but we decided to challenge *you* to come up with creative ideas to meet the needs and abilities of your church, club, or community. Please let us know the clever and wonderful things you do.

Recipes
(*Sister-Tested, Mother Approved!*)

"For the happy heart, life is a continual feast."
Proverbs 15:15

No matter how small or grand the house, everyone always gathers in the kitchen. That's because the way to our hearts is through our stomachs, and because there is something special about that warm, busy place and the smell of spices and good things to eat. Such happy times. Such happy memories. Create some new memories today and have fun cooking for each other and with each other in a sisterly celebration. Bon appetit!

• Soups & Appetizers & Beverages •

Watermelon Pickles (Chapter 7: *A Place to Belong*)
Alright you canners out there, have at it. These are wonderful. Nancy's mother, Marge Young, makes these — and Nancy eats them.

- *1 large watermelon*

Pare and discard the hard dark green rind and trim off the soft pale pink of the rind. Cut pieces of the white rind about 1 inch by 1 inch and ¼ inch to 1/3 inch thick — or whatever size pickles you prefer.

Cover rind with hot water and boil until it's tender and translucent. Drain well, discard the water, and place rind in heat-resistant dish.

Brine:
- *7 cups sugar*
- *2 cups vinegar*

- ½ teaspoon oil of cloves
- ½ teaspoon oil of cinnamon
- 1 teaspoon salt
- 1 lemon, thinly sliced

Combine ingredients in a large pot and bring to a boil. Pour over the rind. Cover and let stand overnight. Repeat the process for three successive days—drain off the brine, bring it to a boil again, and pour over the drained rind. On the third day, pour into mason jars and seal while hot.

• • •

Spinach Dip (Chapter 12: 'Round the Corner)
Great with crackers or veggies.

- 1 package Knorr vegetable soup mix (no substitutions)
- 1 small can water chestnuts (see Asian section of grocery store), chopped
- one 12-ounce package frozen spinach
- 3 tablespoons dried minced onion
- 1 cup fat-free sour cream
- 1 cup fat-free mayo

Thaw the spinach. Squeeze spinach dry—just as it implies, take a glob in your hand and squeeze the liquid out of it. (Take your frustration out!) Mix ingredients. Chill 3 hours.

• • •

Split Pea Soup (Chapter 1: 'Round the Corner)
Great served with Mexican food and chips.

- 1 bag dried green peas
- 6 cups hot water
- 1 ham hock
- several generous drops of liquid smoke
- 3 tablespoons minced onion (dried)

- ½ teaspoon cayenne pepper
- ½ teaspoon crushed red pepper
- 1 bay leaf
- ½ teaspoon thyme
- 1 tablespoon parsley
- salt to taste

Soak the peas overnight; then drain and rinse. Bring all ingredients to a boil, then simmer 3 to 4 hours. Remove bay leaf and ham hock bone before serving.

• • •

Spiced Cider (Chapter 20: *An Undivided Heart*)
Call this Wassail and sing "Oh, here we come a wassailing . . ."

- 1 gallon apple cider
- 2 teaspoons whole allspice
- 2 teaspoons whole cloves
- two 3-inch sticks cinnamon
- 2/3 cup sugar
- orange slices, studded with cloves

Heat all but orange slices to boiling; reduce heat. Cover and simmer 20 minutes. Strain spices and pour into punch bowl. Float orange slices. Makes thirty-two ½-cup servings.

• • •

Tangy Fruit Punch (Chapter 10: *A Place to Belong*)
Dump and stir. Can't get much easier than that!

- 1 can (46 ounces) pineapple juice
- 1 can (12 ounces) thawed orange juice concentrate
- ¾ cup lemonade concentrate
- 1 cup water, divided
- ½ cup sugar

- *2 large, ripe bananas*
- *1 package (20 ounces) frozen unsweetened whole strawberries, thawed*
- *one 2-liter bottle ginger ale or Sprite, chilled*

In a punch bowl or large container, combine juices, sugar, and ½ cup water. Place fruit and remaining water in a blender, cover and process until smooth. Stir into the juice mixture. Cover and refrigerate. Just before serving, add ginger ale. Makes 25 to 30 servings, about 5 quarts.

• • •

Cheese Olives (Chapter 3: *An Undivided Heart*)
Green olives wrapped with a cheesy dough. Yum.

- *½ stick butter, melted*
- *1 small jar cheese spread or 3 inches of processed cheese, melted*
- *¾ cup flour*
- *1 jar green olives, drained*

Mix butter, cheese, and flour. With fingers make a 1-inch circle of dough. Wrap around an olive and pinch shut. Chill until cooled and then bake 20 minutes at 350 degrees.

• • •

Vonette's Taco Soup (Chapter 10: *The Sister Circle*)
Vonette made this for Brenda and Nancy while we were working on the first novel. Seconds of this soup are mandatory!

- *2 large cans tomatoes*
- *1 can white beans*
- *1 can kidney beans*
- *1 can red beans*
- *1 package taco seasoning*

- *1 package ranch dressing seasoning*
- *½ bag frozen corn*

Puree tomatoes (including liquid from can) with the spices. Add drained beans and corn. Cook over low heat or in crockpot and serve.

• • •

Hot Artichoke Dip (Chapter 1: *The Sister Circle*)
Even if you don't usually like artichokes, you'll like this.

- *½ cup mayo*
- *½ cup sour cream*
- *one 14-ounce can artichoke hearts, drained and chopped*
- *1/3 cup grated parmesan cheese*
- *1/8 teaspoon hot pepper sauce (Tabasco)*

Mix together all ingredients. Put in a pie tin or quiche casserole. Bake 30 minutes at 350 degrees or until bubbly. Serve with chunks of bread or crackers.

If you want to make this recipe a bit lighter, use low-fat mayo and sour cream.

• Breads •

Southern Corn Bread (Chapter 13: *'Round the Corner*)
This is great corn bread with real corn in it.

- *1 cup yellow cornmeal*
- *1 cup flour*
- *¼ cup sugar*
- *4 teaspoons baking powder*
- *½ teaspoon salt*
- *1 cup milk*
- *¼ cup oil*
- *1 egg*
- *12 ounces Can Shoe Peg white corn, drained*

In large bowl, combine cornmeal, flour, sugar, baking powder, and salt. Add milk, oil, egg, and corn. Stir just until dry ingredients are moistened. Pour into a greased 9x9-inch pan. Bake for 18 to 23 minutes at 400 degrees. Serve with honey and butter.

• • •

Garlic Cheese Bread (Chapter 8: *'Round the Corner*)
A staple around the Moser house.

- *1 loaf French or Italian crusty bread*
- *butter*
- *garlic salt*
- *shredded Romano or Asiago cheese*

Cut bread into 1- to 1½-inch slices. Place on cookie sheet. Butter and sprinkle with garlic salt. Top with cheese. Broil until browned.

• • •

Lemon Poppy-Seed Muffins (Chapter 9: *'Round the Corner*)
Nancy's favorite. Forget the main dish, she'll just have these.

- 1 1/3 cups flour
- 2/3 cup sugar
- 2 tablespoons poppy seeds
- ¾ teaspoon baking powder
- ¼ teaspoon baking soda
- 1 beaten egg
- 1/3 cup butter, melted
- 2 teaspoons lemon peel
- 3 tablespoons lemon juice
- ½ cup buttermilk (or powdered, made per directions)

In medium bowl mix flour, sugar, poppy seed, baking powder, and baking soda. Make a well in the center of dry ingredients.

In another medium bowl combine egg, butter, lemon peel, and juice. Add buttermilk and stir until combined. Add egg mixture all at once to the dry ingredients. Stir just until moistened (batter should be slightly lumpy). Line muffin tins with baking cups, spray cups with cooking spray. Spoon batter into paper cups, filling ⅔ full. Let sit 5 minutes (it makes them crown). Bake 15 minutes at 400 degrees. Makes 10 to 11.

• • •

Buttermilk Biscuits (Chapter 5: *The Sister Circle*)
Serve hot with butter and honey or smothered with sausage gravy.

- 2 cups flour
- 1 tablespoon baking powder
- ¾ teaspoon salt
- ½ teaspoon baking soda
- 5 tablespoons chilled shortening
- 1 cup buttermilk (or powdered buttermilk made per directions)

Sift together flour, baking powder, baking soda, and salt. Using pastry blender or 2 knives, cut shortening into flour mixture until coarse crumbs form. Add buttermilk, tossing with fork until a dough forms. Turn dough onto lightly floured surface. Knead a few times (for flaky biscuits don't over handle). Pat to ¾ inch thick. Using a glass dipped in flour or a biscuit cutter, cut into biscuits. Put 2 inches apart on an ungreased cookie sheet. Keep using dough trimmings until all is used. Brush with butter. Bake 12 to 15 minutes at 425 degrees. Brush again with butter.

• Main Dishes •

Enchilada Casserole (Chapter 9: *The Sister Circle*)
This is a quantity recipe you can freeze for many meals.
Charles Mead gets the credit for this one.
He worked for Nancy's husband
and shamed the women with his cooking.

This recipe can be made in two
10x10-inch aluminum disposable pans and frozen.
Or make one deep, dense 9x13-inch dish that feeds 10-12.

- *3 cans enchilada sauce (mild)*
- *3 pounds hamburger*
- *¼ teaspoon garlic powder*
- *¼ cup chopped green pepper*
- *½ cup onion, finely chopped*
- *12 to 18 small corn tortillas*
- *1½ to 2 bags cheddar jack shredded cheese*
- *1 small can black olives, chopped*

Cook hamburger, garlic, onions, and peppers together. Drain. Add ¼ can of enchilada sauce. In pan/pans spread a small amount of sauce in the bottom. Put 2 cans of sauce in a bowl and dip tortillas in it, layer in pan, using lots of tortillas (overlapping circles). Layer tortillas, meat, cheese, repeating layers until all used. Put black olives on top and pour rest of sauce (plus one unused can) on top. Use one pan immediately and freeze one. Bake uncovered 30 to 40 minutes at 350 degrees. Let set 10 minutes. To make frozen, must thaw first, then bake. Great to use as a dip too.

• • •

Taco Salad (Chapter 5: *An Undivided Heart*)
Feeds 6 to 8 and is fast and easy.
This is one of Nancy's mother-in-law's recipes: Bev Moser.

- *1 bag lettuce*
- *1 can kidney beans, drained*
- *1 pound hamburger, browned, and cooked in taco seasoning*
- *1 tomato, diced*
- *1 small can sliced black olives*
- *1 cup shredded cheddar cheese*
- *¾ bag nacho-flavored chips, crushed*
- *1 bottle fat-free Catalina dressing*

Do not mix ahead of time. When ready to serve, put all the ingredients together. Leftovers don't work as the dressing makes things mushy. Besides, it's so good you won't have any!

• • •

Burritos (Chapter 9: *An Undivided Heart*)
Need something fast? Need something now? 30 minutes . . .

- *1 pound hamburger, browned, drained*
- *1 can refried beans*
- *1 can Rotel tomatoes with green chilies, drained.*
Mix together and put on flour tortillas.

Add:
- *2 to 3 tablespoons sour cream*
- *1 cup shredded lettuce*
- *1 small can black olives*

Roll up and put on top:
- *mild taco sauce*
- *shredded cheddar or Mexican cheese*
Broil tortillas until cheese melts and serve.

• • •

Waimanalo Ribs (Chapter 5: *The Sister Circle*)
Aloha! Stick a hibiscus in your hair and you're set.
This is from Nancy's Mom, Marge Young.

* *5 pounds country style ribs*

Cover with cold water, and boil 1 hour. Drain. Trim off excess fat.

Heat:
* *1 cup soy sauce*
* *¼ cup prepared mustard*
* *1 cup pineapple juice (or 4 ounces crushed pineapple)*
* *1 clove garlic minced (or ¼ teaspoon powdered garlic)*
* *½ teaspoon ground ginger*

Place boiled ribs in large baking pan. Separate pieces and cover with sauce. Marinate in refrigerator several hours or overnight. Turn occasionally. Bake 30 to 45 minutes at 325 degrees until bubbly.

• • •

Bev's Chili (Chapter 9: *The Sister Circle*)
Nancy's mother-in-law, Bev, gave her this one, too.
Easy, makes a ton, and is the best chili Nancy's ever had.

* *1½ pounds hamburger, browned and drained*
* *2 cans chili with beans*
* *2 cans red beans*
* *2 cans kidney beans*
* *2 cans chili beans*
* *1 envelope chili seasoning*
* *1 quart tomato juice*

Put all ingredients in crockpot or stove top and heat.

• • •

Mae's Manicotti (Chapter 1: *The Sister Circle*)
Quantity and quality! This is a make-ahead dish you can freeze and use for many meals. And actually, it's not Mae's, it's from Nancy's good friend Katy Raymond — who reminds her of Mae...
Here's a great recipe for your freezer!

Mix in a big bowl:
* *1 pound shredded mozzarella*
* *24 ounces cottage cheese*
* *4 eggs*

Mix in another bowl:
* *2 pounds hamburger, browned and drained*
* *three 25-ounce cans spaghetti sauce*

Get out:
* *2 boxes manicotti (28)*

Put some sauce in the bottom of the pans. Fill *un*cooked manicotti shells with cheese mixture (your hands work best). Lay manicotti on the sauced bottom. Cover with more sauce. Note: Make sure the pasta is covered with sauce because the sauce helps it cook, and uncovered pasta gets hard). Drop any leftover cheese mixture on top. Freeze. Makes 3 to 4 pans. Make up various pan sizes of this recipe (most people eat 1 or 2 manicotti). Use aluminum pans you can freeze and won't miss having around. To make: Thaw. Bake 1½ hours at 350 degrees.

• • •

Monte Cristo Sandwiches (Chapter 18: *An Undivided Heart*)
The beauty of this sandwich is its versatility.
It can be served to men as a substantial meal or to an elegant luncheon cut into smaller servings.
Brenda prefers sourdough bread to best support the egg dip.

To make 4 sandwiches:
- *Lightly butter 8 slices of bread.*
- *Place slices of sliced turkey and ham on 4 slices.*
- *Add a slice of mozzarella cheese.*
- *Top with remaining slices of bread.*

Prepare an egg mixture. Beat:
- *2 eggs*
- *¼ cup milk*
- *2 teaspoons flour*
- *¼ teaspoon salt*

Dip each sandwich into the egg mixture and saturate both sides. Fry on a griddle pan or large skillet until golden. Cut diagonally and dust with powdered sugar. Serve with raspberry jam. (Yes, raspberry jam!)

• • •

Smothered Steak (Chapter 17: 'Round the Corner)
This takes a while, but it's a low-maintenance dish once it's cooking.
A Moser meal.

- *Round steak, cut into individual servings, fat removed*
- *flour*
- *paprika*

Dip steaks in flour and paprika, and fry in pan until lightly brown. Remove to a plate. Drain grease. Add a few tablespoons of flour and 2 to 3 cups of water to make a lot of gravy. Return meat to pan, cover with gravy, and cook covered 2 hours on low. Add mushrooms if you like.

• • •

Chipped Beef on Toast (Chapter 17: 'Round the Corner)
Ah, come on. It may not be fancy, but it's good.

- *2 tablespoons butter or butter*
- *2 tablespoons flour*
- *2 cups milk*
- *one 4-ounce package of chipped beef*
- *salt and pepper to taste*

Melt butter in saucepan over medium heat. Stir in flour until smooth and heat until bubbly. Gradually stir in milk to keep it from getting lumpy. The mixture — which is a white sauce — will gradually thicken. Tear the beef into small pieces and add to sauce, cooking over low heat about 5 minutes. Add salt and pepper as desired. Serve over toast. Serves 4 — or 2 if you let yourself get into it.

• • •

Stovetop Alfredo (Chapter 6: 'Round the Corner)
Kids love this one, and it isn't fattening like real alfredo sauce.

- *1½ cups water*
- *½ cup milk*
- *2 tablespoons butter*
- *1 package alfredo noodles & sauce mix*
- *16-ounce package frozen vegetables (peas or else a corn broccoli mix)*
- *1½ cups cubed ham, or Spam (even shaved ham will do in a pinch)*

In saucepan, combine water, milk, butter. Bring to boil. Stir in noodles, sauce mix, vegetables, and ham. Cook over medium heat 6 to 8 minutes.

• • •

Gingered Flank Steak (Chapter 1: *A Place to Belong*)
Great taste, pretty, and easy (though you do have to think ahead).

- *1½ pounds lean beef flank steak*
- *1/3 cup lemon juice*
- *2 tablespoons honey*
- *1 teaspoon soy sauce*
- *1 teaspoon ginger*
- *2 cloves garlic (or garlic powder)*

Trim fat from steak. Cut both sides of beef into diamond design, 1/8″ deep. Place meat in shallow dish. Mix other ingredients. Pour over beef. Cover and refrigerate at least 8 hours, turning occasionally. Broil or grill (spray pan or grill with cooking spray). *Keep the marinade,* and use it to baste meat while grilling.

• • •

Yummy Roast (Chapter 4: *The Sister Circle*)
This crock pot dish is from Nancy's sister, Crys Mach.

- *1 package au jus seasoning mix*
- *1 package Italian salad dressing mix*
- *1 can beef broth*
- *1 roast*
- *potatoes and/or carrots*
- *mushroom gravy mix*
- *fresh mushrooms*

Put seasonings, beef broth, and roast in crockpot all day with water to cover roast. Add potatoes and vegetables during last hour. Make gravy using juice from crockpot by first sautéing fresh mushrooms in butter. Then boiling meat juice, thickening it with cornstarch

• • •

Elegant Meat Loaf (Chapter 12: *'Round the Corner*)
If you have leftovers (very unlikely), slice the meatloaf and make sandwiches on marble rye bread with shredded cabbage and pickles.

- *2 pounds lean ground beef*
- *1 cup oatmeal*
- *1 tablespoon dried onion flakes*
- *2 eggs, slightly beaten*
- *1½ teaspoons salt*
- *½ teaspoon coarse ground pepper*
- *2 tablespoons Worcestershire sauce*
- *½ teaspoon Cajun spices (adds zip)*

Combine all ingredients. Press into a loaf pan or shape as a roll and bake at 350 degrees for 45 minutes.

Now for the topping:
- *onion sliced and sautéed in small amount of oil*

Then add:
- *½ cup brown sugar*
- *¼ cup Dijon mustard*
- *1 cup ketchup*

Ladle over sliced meatloaf and feel fancy.

• • •

Easy Goulash (Chapter 7: *The Sister Circle*)
This is Super-Easy category and tastes even better warmed up later.

- *1 large can tomato juice*
- *1 pound hamburger, cooked and drained*
- *2 cups dry macaroni*

Cook on stovetop at medium for 45-60 minutes until macaroni is soft (stir occasionally). Add salt and pepper to taste.

• • •

Bestest Ever Lasagna (Chapter 1: *The Sister Circle* and Chapter 4: *'Round the Corner*)
Forgive the bad grammar in its name, it IS the bestest!

- *3 pounds hamburger*
- *4 garlic cloves, minced*
- *2 jars spaghetti sauce (like Ragu or Prego)*
- *1 box lasagna noodles, cooked and drained*
- *2-16 oz. cartons small curd cottage cheese*
- *4 cups (16 ounces) shredded mozzarella cheese*

Preheat oven to 350.
Prepare the lasagna noodles (boil 12-14 minutes).
In a large sauce pan, cook beef and garlic over medium heat. Drain. Add spaghetti sauce. Cover and simmer 30 minutes. (Or put it in a crockpot to keep warm until later.)
Spray a 9 x 13 with Pam. Put 3 noodles in bottom. Add ¼ of the hamburger mixture, ¼ of the cottage cheese, ¼ of the mozzarella. Repeat three more times. Bake 30-40 minutes at 350 degrees. Let stand 10 minutes before cutting. Serves 12.

• • •

Swedish Meat Balls (Chapter 6: *The Sister Circle*)
The allspice makes these different.
From Nancy's Minnesota Swedish roots . . .

- *1 pound hamburger*
- *½ cup fine bread crumbs, or 1 cup torn up bread*
- *1 teaspoon allspice*
- *1 tablespoon milk*
- *1 tablespoon dried minced onion*
- *Salt and pepper*

Mix ingredients together and form into firm balls. Put in small baking pan (they can touch). Cook 45 minutes at 375.

• • •

Cranberry Chicken (Chapter 2: *An Undivided Heart*)
Looks like you worked hard . . . we can pretend, can't we?

- *4 to 6 boneless chicken breasts*
- *one 8-ounce bottle French dressing*
- *1 can solid cranberry sauce*
- *1 packet onion soup mix*

Put all ingredients in 9x13 pan. Bake at 375 degrees for 1 hour, covered. Serve with rice, made separately.

• • •

Chicken Pasta Salad with Spicy Peanut Sauce
(Chapter 12: *A Place to Belong*)
This is a nice lunch to make for your girlfriends.
It's pretty too and makes enough for 4-6.

Sauce:
- *¼ cup minced onion (fresh, not dried)*
- *1 tablespoon peanut oil*
- *1/3 cup chicken broth*
- *¼ cup peanut butter*
- *1 tablespoon soy sauce*
- *1 teaspoon lime juice*
- *½ teaspoon ground coriander*
- *¼ teaspoon hot pepper sauce*
- *¼ teaspoon crushed red pepper (only if you like it spicy!)*

Sauté onion in oil until limp but not browned. Stir in remaining ingredients. Mixture may be prepared several hours ahead. Store in refrigerator up to 2 days. Bring to room temperature to serve.

Salad:
- *¾ pound boneless chicken breast (cooked; chill until used)*

- *½ pound pasta (your choice)*
- *1 tablespoon peanut oil*
- *½ cup slivered red bell pepper*
- *½ cup slivered snow peas*
- *½ cup slivered carrots*
- *2 tablespoons chopped roasted peanuts*

Cook pasta. Drain and toss gently with 1 tablespoon peanut oil. Heat the peanut oil and stir fry the veggies. Place pasta on plates and top with veggies and diagonally sliced chicken. Top with peanuts. Pass the sauce.

• • •

Fontina Chicken (Chapter 8: *'Round the Corner*
and Chapter 11: *An Undivided Heart*)
*Nancy created this after being inspired
by a dish at Carrabba's.
It may be her only cooking creation that's ever turned out.*

- *4 boneless, skinless chicken breasts*
- *4 slices Canadian bacon*
- *4 slices Fontina cheese (a mild white cheese)*

Brown chicken breasts. Slice like a sandwich and insert piece of bacon and cheese. Broil until cheese melts.

For gravy:
- *2 tablespoons butter*
- *2 tablespoons flour*
- *¼ teaspoon salt*
- *1 cup boiling water*
- *1 chicken bouillon cube (or 1 cup canned chicken broth)*
- *¼ cup butter*
- *½ pound sliced mushrooms.*
- *1 teaspoon basil*

Melt 2 tablespoons butter in saucepan. Add flour and salt,

and heat until bubbly. Add water and bullion and cook, stirring constantly until thickened. In another saucepan, heat ¼ cup butter. Add mushrooms and cook until tender — not brown. Stir mushrooms in gravy. Serve over chicken breasts.

• • •

Chicken Spaghetti (Chapter 4: *A Place to Belong*)
This recipe freezes well and is easy to serve.
Nancy sings in an octet. While singing in Arkansas, they stayed (and were fed) at the home of Nancy and Hal Savage.

- *6 pounds chicken*
- *8 ribs celery*
- *3 medium onions*
- *2 carrots*
- *1 stick butter*
- *1 large green pepper*
- *1 large can stewed tomatoes*
- *one 15-ounce can tomato sauce*
- *1 pound spaghetti*
- *½ pound grated cheese (cheddar, Swiss, your choice)*
- *1 small jar pimentos*
- *1 small can ripe olives*
- *1 large can mushrooms*

Simmer chicken with 2 ribs of celery, 2 carrots, and one onion in 2 cups of water until easily boned. Meanwhile, sauté in one stick of butter the remaining 6 ribs of chopped celery, 1 chopped green pepper, and 2 medium chopped onions. Add stewed tomatoes and can of tomato sauce.

Simmer till chicken tender. Remove it from broth to cool for deboning, discard vegetables that cooked with chicken and boil broth down to 1 to 1¼ cups. Thicken with flour for a very thick gravy.

Cook spaghetti in water. Drain. Pour gravy over the spaghetti. Add chicken, tomatoes, cheese, olives, pimentos, and mushrooms. Bake 1 hour at 325. Uncover last 15 minutes.

• Salads & Veggies •

Hash Brown Casserole (Chapter 11: *'Round the Corner*)
This recipe comes from Nancy's daughter-in-law, Mallory.
There won't be any leftovers. Guaranteed.

- *2 pounds frozen shredded potatoes or hash browns*
- *2 cups sour cream*
- *1 can cream of chicken soup*
- *2 cups shredded cheddar cheese*
- *1 small diced onion*
- *1 teaspoon salt*
- *¼ cup melted butter*
- *2 cups crushed cornflakes*

Combine all but cornflakes & butter. Put in greased 9x13-inch pan. Bake 45 minutes at 375. During the last 15 minutes, put crushed corn flakes (mixed with melted butter) on top.

• • •

Peach Fluff (Chapter 4: *The Sister Circle*)
You can use either peach or apricot products. A luscious looking (and tasting) salad from Nancy's sister-in-law, Deanna Brown.

- *1 large package peach Jell-O (you can use Sugar-Free)*
- *1¼ cups boiling water*
- *1 large can peaches*
- *8 ounces cream cheese (you can use 1/3 or Fat-free)*

Put Jell-O powder and water in blender. Mix well. Add peaches (and juice) and cream cheese (you might have to blend it in shifts as it makes a lot). Chill until firm.

• • •

Applesauce Red Hots Salad (Chapter 1: *A Place to Belong*)
We cheer for any recipe that uses candy.

- *1 cup water*
- *¼ cup red hots (the candy)*
- *1 small package strawberry Jell-O*
- *1 cup fine applesauce*

Heat the water and red hots together until candy melts. Add the Jell-O and applesauce. Chill until firm.

• • •

Mandarin Orange Salad (Chapter 5: *The Sister Circle*)
The combination of spicy and sweet is wonderful.
Make the dressing just to have around for other lettuce salads.

- *3 green onions*
- *1 package mixed lettuce*
- *1 can mandarin oranges (drained)*
- *1 carton berries or canned pineapple tidbits*
- *1 handful of dried cranberries*
- *1 small package sliced almonds*
- *1 tablespoon sugar*
- *1 tablespoon butter*

Dressing:
- *½ cup vegetable oil*
- *4 tablespoons red wine or cider or raspberry vinegar*
- *4 tablespoons sugar*
- *1 teaspoon salt*
- *5 to 6 drops Tabasco sauce*

Sauté almonds in 1 tablespoon sugar and 1 tablespoon butter until golden. Cool. Mix all dressing ingredients in a cruet and chill. Toss salad and fruit with dressing just prior to serving. Save a few almonds to garnish the top of the salad.

• Breakfasts •

Sausage and Grits Casserole (Chapter 4: *An Undivided Heart*)
Not being Southerners, we didn't know about grits.
But we do now! This is another one of Nancy Savage's recipes.

- *1 pound mild ground sausage*
- *3 servings instant grits prepared according to package directions*
- *1 stick butter*
- *1 cup shredded Mexican cheese*
- *½ cup milk*
- *3 eggs*
- *Paprika for color on top*

Fry sausage, drain well. Cook grits in boiling, salted water according to package directions. Add butter and cheese and stir until melted. Beat milk and eggs together, then add to hot mixture, stirring constantly. Add sausage and pour in greased 9x13-inch pan. Sprinkle with paprika. Bake at 375 degrees for 45 minutes until browned on top. May be made ahead and frozen before baking. If cold, bake 45 to 60 minutes.

• • •

Mountain Mash Oatmeal (Chapter 10: *An Undivided Heart*)
Nancy first had this at Brenda's house. Nummy, nummy.
It was first served to Brenda at the home of Al and Hermine Hartley.
Al was one of the original illustrators for the Archie Comic series.
(Are you a Veronica or a Betty?)

- *oatmeal (not instant)*
- *Granny smith apples (chop up and zap in microwave to soften)*
- *walnuts*
- *dried cranberries*
- *raisins*

- *cinnamon*
- *milk*
- *brown sugar*

Cook oatmeal per package directions. Add your choice of toppings. Serve with milk and brown sugar.

• • •

Applesauce Pancakes (Chapter 4: *'Round the Corner* and Chapter 18: *An Undivided Heart*)
These are moist inside so cook them long enough. The recipe comes from Curtis Westbrook, a college friend of Nancy's son, Carson.

- *1 cup flour*
- *2 teaspoons baking powder*
- *¼ teaspoon salt*
- *1 egg*
- *1 tablespoon melted butter*
- *½ jar applesauce*
- *2 teaspoons cinnamon*
- *up to 1 cup milk*

Mix all ingredients but milk. Add just enough milk to make it into a thick but pourable batter. Ladle onto medium hot griddle sprayed with Pam. Cook until brown on both sides — don't undercook. Makes 7, 4-inch pancakes. Serve with syrup.

• • •

French Toast Casserole (Chapter 10: *An Undivided Heart*)
Another recipe from Nancy Savage. Who needs lunch? Give me a double helping for breakfast!

- *1 cup brown sugar*
- *1 loaf French bread*
- *½ cup butter, melted*

- *3 teaspoons cinnamon*
- *6 eggs*
- *3 tart apples, peeled, cored, sliced*
- *1½ cups milk*
- *½ cup dried cranberries*
- *1 tablespoon vanilla*

Combine sugar, butter, and 1 teaspoon cinnamon in 9x13-inch pan. Add fruit, toss to coat well. Spread evenly. Arrange slices of bread on top. Mix egg, milk, vanilla and 2 teaspoons cinnamon. Pour over bread. Cover and refrigerate 4 to 24 hours.

Cover with aluminum foil sprayed with cooking spray (so it won't stick). Bake at 375 degrees for 40 minutes. Uncover and bake 5 minutes more. Remove from oven and let stand 5 minutes. You can use blueberries instead of cranberries, but increase the amount to 1 cup.

• • •

Betty's Coffee Cake (Chapter 5: *The Sister Circle*)
A favorite. "Betty" is Nancy's Aunt Betty in Fargo, North Dakota. Uff-da.

- *1½ cups sugar*
- *½ cup shortening*
- *2 eggs*
- *1 cup milk*
- *3 cups flour*
- *1 tablespoon baking powder*
- *1 teaspoon salt*

Crumb mixture: (you can double the crumble if you want)
- *1 cup brown sugar*
- *4 tablespoons flour*
- *6 teaspoon cinnamon*
- *1 cup raisins*
- *4 tablespoons melted butter or butter*

Mix the sugar, shortening, and eggs together. Then stir in the milk, flour, baking powder, and salt. Pour into a greased 8½x11-inch baking pan. Combine the brown sugar, 4 tablespoons flour, cinnamon, raisins, and butter to make crumb mixture.

Sprinkle crumb mixture over top. Bake 40 to 45 minutes at 325 degrees or until brown on top and not gooey inside. Serve with butter. (Good the next day, too. Slice a piece horizontally, slip in some butter, and reheat piece by piece in the microwave. Then go back for seconds.)

• Sweets •

Lemon Cool-Whip Cookies (Chapter 10: *A Place to Belong*)
Don't you love recipes that only have five ingredients?

- *1 package lemon cake mix*
- *1¾ cups Cool Whip*
- *3 tablespoons oil*
- *1 egg*
- *sugar and colored sugar*

In large bowl combine cake mix, Cool Whip, oil and egg. Mix. Cover and chill dough one hour. Shape dough into 1-inch balls, and roll in sugar. Place 2 inches apart on greased cookie sheets. Bake 10 to 12 minutes at 350 degrees or until golden brown around edges. Allow cookies to cool 1 minute before removing from cookie sheets. Cool completely.

For colored sugar: Add a few drops food coloring to sugar. Whisk it to separate.

• • •

Chocolate Drop Cookies (Chapter 11: *'Round the Corner*)
A favorite of Nancy's husband. A sure way to his heart.

- *2 cups sugar*
- *½ cup cocoa*
- *¼ cup butter*
- *½ cup milk*
- *½ cup peanut butter*
- *3 to 3 ½ cups oatmeal*

Melt all but oatmeal, stirring constantly. Add the oatmeal. Spoon out on waxed paper. Let cool.

• • •

Fruit Cocktail Cake (Chapter 3: *'Round the Corner*)
*Nancy used to do a lot in community theater. This recipe is from a
cast mate, Terri. The frosting is great on devil's food cake, too.*

- *3 cups flour*
- *2 ¼ cups sugar*
- *½ teaspoon baking soda*
- *½ teaspoon salt*
- *3 beaten eggs*
- *2 regular sized cans fruit cocktail – undrained*

Mix ingredients, and put in greased 9x13 pan. Bake 40 to
45 minutes at 300 degrees.

Broiled Coconut Frosting:
- *1 stick butter*
- *1½ cups coconut*
- *½ cup milk*
- *1 cup brown sugar*
- *1 teaspoon vanilla*

Cook 2 minutes. Pour over cake. Broil until light brown.

• • •

Apple Brown Betty (Chapter 1: *'Round the Corner*)
*Think of cool days, falling leaves, reading a book in a cozy chair,
the smell of cinnamon wafting through the house.
Who's hungry now?*

- *1 cup fresh bread crumbs*
- *¼ cup brown sugar, packed*
- *½ teaspoon cinnamon*
- *¼ teaspoon nutmeg*
- *¼ teaspoon cloves*
- *4 tablespoons butter*
- *2 pounds tart sweet apples (about 3 large)*

- *2 tablespoons lemon juice*
- *1/3 cup chopped walnuts or pecans*

Preheat the broiler. Spread the bread crumbs on a cookie sheet and toast until golden, turning so they color evenly. Set aside.

Mix sugar with the spices. Cut the butter into pea-size pieces and set aside. Peel, core, and slice the apples. Toss with lemon juice to prevent browning. Sprinkle 3 tablespoons of bread crumbs over the bottom of a greased 2 quart casserole. Cover with one-third of the apples and sprinkle with one-third of the sugar-spice mixture. Add another layer of bread crumbs and dot with one-third of the butter. Repeat the layers two more times, ending with a layer of bread crumbs. Sprinkle with the nuts and dot with remaining butter. Bake 35 to 40 minutes at 375 degrees.

• • •

Apple Pie (Chapter 8: *'Round the Corner*)
*The smell and sight of an apple pie has been known to sell real estate,
encourage marriage proposals, and definitely impress in-laws.
Brenda's sister-in-law, Jolane, convinced her
that baking a pie didn't have to be an all-day event.
The secret is store-bought sheets of pie crust dough.*

- *Pillsbury pie crust sheets (2)*
- *6 large, firm, tart apples*
- *1 ½ tablespoons flour*
- *1 cup sugar*
- *½ teaspoon salt*
- *1 teaspoon cinnamon*
- *½ teaspoon nutmeg*
- *½ teaspoon allspice*
- *2 tablespoons butter*

Preheat the oven to 350 degrees. Put one crust in a greased pie pan. Mix the dry ingredients and add the drained apple slices. Place in the pie crust. Add butter to the top of the apples. Lay the top crust over the apples and crimp the edges with fingers or fork. To achieve a beautiful crust, brush with egg white and sprinkle with sugar before baking. Bake 50 minutes at 350 degrees or until done. A tiny heart shaped cookie cutter makes a great design and provides the needed vents for baking.

• • •

Carrot Cake (Chapter 20: *An Undivided Heart*)
Yes, that's baby food in there . . . Sister-in-law Sheree Moser came up with this one. It's incredibly moist.

- *2 cups sugar*
- *1 cup vegetable oil*
- *4 eggs*
- *2 cups flour*
- *1½ teaspoons soda*
- *½ teaspoon salt*
- *3 teaspoons cinnamon*
- *4 junior jars carrot baby food*

Bake 35 to 40 minutes at 350 degrees. Do not over bake.

Frosting:

- *8 ounces fat-free cream cheese, at room temperature*
- *2 cups powdered sugar*
- *1 teaspoon vanilla*
- *2 teaspoons butter, at room temperature*

Mix ingredients together. Generously frost cake.

• • •

Pumpkin Pie (Chapter14: *'Round the Corner*)
This is Brenda's dressed-up version of a holiday favorite.
Try serving this pie on a hot summer day with iced tea.

- *Frozen pie crust for 9-inch pie, thawed*
- *1 cup sugar*
- *½ teaspoon salt*
- *1½ teaspoons cinnamon*
- *½ teaspoon powdered ginger*
- *½ teaspoon ground cloves*
- *1½ cups canned pumpkin*
- *1½ cups evaporated milk*
- *2 eggs slightly beaten*
- *whipped cream (or Cool Whip)*
- *caramel ice cream topping*

Preheat the oven to 425 degrees. Mix all ingredients except whipped cream and caramel ice cream topping, and pour filling into the pie crust. Bake for 10 minutes, then lower the heat to 300 degrees and bake for about 45 minutes or until the filling is firm.

When you are ready to serve your chilled pie, cover the top with whipped cream sealing the edges (forget the idea of a dollop and frost the pie like a cake). After each piece is on a plate drizzle the pie and plate with caramel ice cream topping (pour the caramel into a plastic sandwich bag, and snip a tiny corner off the bag to create your drizzle). Be creative with your drizzles. Sounds like a life lesson, doesn't it?

• • •

Pistachio Dessert (Chapter 10: *A Place to Belong*)
Luscious. You'll want to eat the whole thing!

- *2 to 3 cups crushed graham crackers*
- *½ cup butter, melted*
- *8 ounces fat-free cream cheese, softened*
- *1 cup powdered sugar*

- *8 ounces Cool Whip*
- *two 3.75-ounce packages pistachio instant pudding*
- *3 cups milk*

Melt butter and mix with graham crackers. Press into 9x13-inch pan. In a small bowl, combine cream cheese and powdered sugar until smooth and creamy. Fold in ½ carton of Cool Whip, spread over cooled crust. In medium bowl, combine pudding mix and milk, beat thoroughly. Pour carefully over cheese layer. Frost with remaining Cool Whip. Refrigerate several hours or overnight. 12 servings.

• • •

Perfect Cheesecake (Chapter 5: *The Sister Circle*
and Chapter 4: *'Round the Corner*)
*Nancy is not a great cook yet this always turns out,
so it deserves its title.
This is the cheesecake she often makes for big family dinners.
To make it fancy serve with cherry pie filling
and Hershey's syrup in a little glass pitcher.*

Important Hints (because perfection is tricky):
- *start with ingredients at room temperature*
- *beat the cheese and sugar thoroughly because once the batter thickens, it's impossible to get the lumps out.*
- *Stir the filling gently after adding the eggs. Vigorous beating incorporates too much air, which causes the cheesecake to puff, then fall and crack.*

- *1¾ cups finely crushed graham crackers (1 inner package)*
- *¼ cup finely chopped walnuts*
- *½ teaspoon cinnamon*
- *½ cup butter, melted (1 stick: no substitutes)*
- *three 8-ounce packages light cream cheese, softened (Don't use the fat-free, it doesn't set. Lite is okay.)*
- *1 cup sugar*
- *2 tablespoons flour*

- *1 teaspoon vanilla*
- *2 eggs*
- *1 egg yolk*
- *¼ cup milk*

For crust, in a medium bowl, combine crushed crackers, walnuts, and cinnamon. Stir in melted butter. Press crumb mixture evenly onto the bottom and about 2 inches up the sides of an 8- or 9-inch spring-form pan. (Use the bottom of a measuring cup to press it down.)

For filling: In a large bowl, beat the cream cheese, sugar, flour, and vanilla with a mixer on medium until combined. Add the whole eggs and egg yolk all at once. Beat on low speed just until combined. Stir in milk. Pour the filling into the crust-lined spring-form pan. Place the pan in a shallow baking pan in the oven rack. Bake in a 375-degree oven for 45 to 50 minutes for an 8-inch pan and 35 to 40 minutes for a 9-inch pan or until center appears nearly set when shaken.

Remove spring-form pan from oven-baking pan. Cool cheesecake in spring-form pan on a wire rack for 15 minutes. Use a small metal spatula to loosen crust from sides of pan. Cool 30 minutes more. Remove sides of the spring-form pan. Cool 1 hour, cover and chill at least 4 hours. Serves 12 to 16.

• • •

Strawberry-Kiwi Meringues (Chapter 6: *The Sister Circle*)
These look hard but aren't — and have virtually no calories!

- *2 egg whites*
- *1 teaspoon vanilla*
- *½ teaspoon cream of tartar*
- *¼ teaspoon salt*
- *½ cup sugar*

Line cookie sheet with parchment paper. Beat egg whites until frothy. Add vanilla, cream of tartar, and salt and beat slightly. Gradually add sugar, beating well after each addition.

Beat until stiff peaks are formed when beater is lifted up. Drop 6 large (or 18 small) mounds from spoon onto baking sheet allowing 2 inches between. Hollow out centers to form meringue shells. Bake 1 hour at 250 degrees or until dry to touch. Fill with: pudding, strawberries, kiwis, sherbet . . .

• • •

7-Minute Frosting (Chapter 2: *An Undivided Heart*)
This frosting is amazing. Glossy and thick and lovely.
Nancy's mom used to make it for special occasions.

- *1½ cups sugar*
- *½ cup water*
- *1 tablespoon light corn syrup*
- *⅛ teaspoon salt*
- *2 egg whites, unbeaten*
- *1 teaspoon vanilla*

Combine all ingredients except vanilla, and mix well in top of double boiler. Place over boiling water and immediately beat with rotary beater (while on the stove) 7 to 10 minutes, or until mixture holds stiff peaks. Remove from heat and beat in 1 teaspoon vanilla. You can add food coloring, crushed peppermint candies, Butterfinger crumbles...be creative!

• • •

Easy Mints (Chapter 10: *A Place to Belong*)
This is a Moser recipe. The Mosers often make their own mints
for anniversaries, weddings,
and special events (like a Sister Circle party!)
They freeze nicely. This recipes makes around 75 mints.

- *4 ounces cream cheese*
- *4 cups powdered sugar*
- *½ teaspoon flavoring (strawberry, mint, almond . . .)*
- *Food coloring*

Note: You'll need 1 or 2 *soft* rubber mint molds. (Check craft stores: A rose and a leaf are neat ones. These are *not* the hard clear plastic ones. They need to be pliable so you can pop the mints out one at a time.)

Knead ingredients with bread hook in mixer. Should be the consistency of bread dough. Chill a few hours. Roll in 1-inch balls, then roll balls in regular sugar (make a model ball to use to gauge size. Set on counter). Push ball into mold. Pop out and put on waxed paper. Dry overnight. Flip over. Dry more. Freeze in Tupperware.

• • •

If you aren't full by now . . .
We admire your stamina.

The Sister Circle Novels
(*A Blurb about the Books*)
by Nancy Moser and Vonette Bright

Book 1: *The Sister Circle:* Evelyn Peerbaugh is a widow without funds who is forced to open her Victorian home to boarders: a flamboyant ex-hippie, an elderly Bible teacher, an unwed mother with her child, and a single high school teacher whose goal is to be married with children. Who knew such a diverse group of women could bond like sisters?

Book 2: *'Round the Corner:* Evelyn and the original tenants found a calm cove of sister-hood. Though the water was rough at times, they learned to float. But now Evelyn is starting over with a new set of boarders—one tenant with a chip on her shoulder, and another who likes men a bit too much. Can these women ever be true sisters?

Book 3: *An Undivided Heart:* An old tenant is back in town, love is in the air for sisters old and new, and a new boarder with a penchant for plastic surgery moves in. It's natural she has issues with another new tenant who is a young, fresh-faced beauty who thinks using make-up consists of lip gloss.

Book 4: *A Place to Belong:* The sisters show their faith-in-action to new boarders: a Ukrainian mail-order bride, an old friend in need, and an ambitious writer with an attitude. Peerbaugh Place shines and shows us how we all can find our proper place to belong in God's plan. As the final book in the series, it's plum full of satisfying wrap-ups. Enjoy!

That's it. We're through. But you're not. You have things to do, places to see, and sisters to be. Go do it! God bless us every one!

Let us help you plan your women's event!

God's Gifts Workshop
Your Potential * Your Purpose * His Plan

Enjoy a day of self-discovery that will energize and empower, as you realize the potential of your God-given gifts.

"The greatest fear is not that you will fail, but that you will succeed in doing the wrong thing."
Howard Hendricks

Session #1: Discover YOUR POTENTIAL
Identify the gifts God has given you.
Learn how your abilities complement those around you
and how your combined strengths
can make a powerful impact.

Session #2: Pinpoint YOUR PURPOSE
Utilize your God-Given gifts to set in motion
your unique purpose.
Find the exciting promise of a faith-filled life.

Session #3: Recognize HIS PLAN
Discover how God gives you direction.
Learn to listen to His instructions,
and become all you were meant to be.

GOD'S GIFTS WORKSHOP:
- The format can be a Friday evening and Saturday, or a one-day program.
- We have three one-hour sessions of solid teaching and interact with attendees at breaks and mealtimes.

Book an event or get more information:
Nancy Moser: bookmoser@gmail.com
Brenda Josee: bjosee396@gmail.com

About the Authors

NANCY MOSER lives in Kansas City with her husband, three married children, and seven grandkids. She's an award-winning author of 30 novels. Her genres include both contemporary and historical stories about people discovering their unique purpose. She kills all her houseplants, and can wire an electrical fixture without getting shocked. She is a fan of anything antique — humans included.

See Nancy's website at www.nancymoser.com
Author blog: www.authornancymoser.blogspot.com
History blog: www.footnotesfromhistory.blogspot.com

BRENDA JOSEE lives in California with her husband, a married son and his wife, and two grandchildren. She has been active in Christian Publishing for 40 years, and is currently a literary consultant. She was editor-in-chief of Tapestry magazine, and has worked with Max Lucado, Kay Arthur, and Bill and Vonette Bright. She likes directing other people's lives, and gardening — but who wouldn't in Southern California?

Blog: www.bitsfrombrenda.blogspot.com

The Books of Nancy Moser

Contemporary Books

The Invitation (Book 1 of Mustard Seed Series)
The Quest (Book 2 of Mustard Seed Series)
The Temptation (Book 3 of Mustard Seed Series)
Crossroads
The Seat Beside Me (Book 1 of Steadfast Series)
A Steadfast Surrender (Book 2 of Steadfast Series)
The Ultimatum (Book 3 of Steadfast Series)
The Sister Circle (Book 1 of Sister Circle Series)
Round the Corner (Book 2 of Sister Circle Series)
An Undivided Heart (Book 3 of Sister Circle Series)
A Place to Belong (Book 4 of Sister Circle Series)
The Sister Circle Handbook (Book 5 of Sister Circle Series)
Time Lottery (Book 1 of Time Lottery Series)
Second Time Around (Book 2 of Time Lottery Series)
John 3:16
The Good Nearby
Solemnly Swear

Historical Novels

The Pattern Artist
The Fashion Designer
Love of the Summerfields (Book 1 of Manor House Series)
Bride of the Summerfields (Book 2 of Manor House Series)
Rise of the Sumemrfields (Book 3 of Manor House Series)
Mozart's Sister (biographical novel of Nannerl Mozart)
Just Jane (biographical novel of Jane Austen)
Washington's Lady (bio-novel of Martha Washington)
How Do I Love Thee? (bio-novel of Elizabeth Barrett Browning)
Masquerade
An Unlikely Suitor
The Journey of Josephine Cain
A Patchwork Christmas (novella collection)
A Basket Brigade Christmas (novella collection)
Regency Brides (novella collection)
Christmas Stitches (novella collection)

www.nancymoser.com

Read *Crossroads* by Nancy Moser

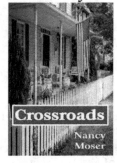

Eighty-one-year-old Madeline stormed into the middle of Weaver's main intersection, positioned herself directly beneath its only traffic light, spread her arms wide, and screamed, "I will not allow it!" Just to make sure every atom and chromosome of every person within range heard her proclamation, she turned one-hundred-and-eighty degrees and did it again. "Do you hear me? I will not allow it!"

The light guiding the traffic traveling along Emma Street turned green, but there was no need for Madeline McHenry Weaver to move out of the way. The light could show its colors from now until Elvis returned and she would not have to move — for safety's sake anyway. Yet the truth was, she couldn't stand out here all day. If the heat of their Indian summer hot-spell didn't get to her, her arthritis would. Annoying thing, getting old.

"You done yet?"

Web Stoddard sat at the corner, on a bench that skirted the town's only park, with one arm draped over its back, his overall-clad legs crossed. The shoelace on his right work boot was untied and teased the sidewalk. He slowly shooed a fly away as if he didn't have anything better to do.

Which he didn't.

Which brought Madeline back to the problem at hand.

She waved her arms expansively, ignoring the light turning red. "No, I'm not done yet. And I won't be done until people start listening to me."

His right ankle danced a figure eight. "No people to hear, Maddy. It's too late."

She stomped a foot. "It's not too late! It can't be."

Web nodded to the Weaver Mercantile opposite the bench. "Want to go sit at the soda fountain? I have a key."

"You have a key to every empty business in town. Don't abuse the privilege."

He nodded slowly, then grinned. "Want to go neck in the back of the hardware store?"

She crunched up her nose. "It smells like varnish and nails in there."

"Not a bad smell."

(Read more www.nancymoser.com/excerptcrossroads)